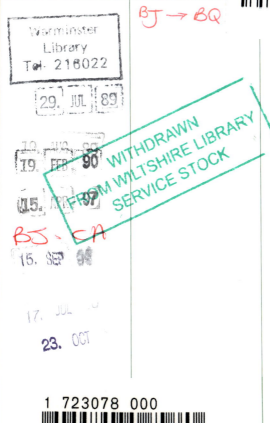

Strindberg's
THE FATHER
and
Ibsen's
HEDDA GABLER

Adapted by
JOHN OSBORNE

faber and faber
LONDON · BOSTON

First published in 1989
by Faber and Faber Limited
3 Queen Square London WC1N 3AU
Hedda Gabler was first published in a
single volume in 1972

Photoset by Wilmaset, Birkenhead, Wirral
Printed in Great Britain by
Richard Clay Ltd, Bungay, Suffolk
All rights reserved

British Library Cataloguing in Publication Data
is available

ISBN 0-571-14066-1

CONTENTS

THE FATHER
by
August Strindberg

INTRODUCTION

In July 1988 I was asked by the National Theatre to produce a new English version of *The Father*. My immediate response was to refuse. For one thing, after having worked on an adaptation of *Hedda Gabler* some years before, during a far more fugitive period of my life, I was disinclined.

It seemed to me that adaptations of this kind, often of 'unperformed European masterpieces', were best left to academics and those who have at least a linguistic familiarity with the intricacies and translation puzzles of works originally written in a tongue familiar to few. Besides, apart from the constant appeals of theatrical journalists, hot-foot from the base camps of dramatic literature with their discoveries, these unperformed masterpieces had remained unperformed for one reason. They were, in the words of my old friend, George Devine, 'bloody boring', of no interest to anyone except professional theatre critics, desperate for some respite from their one hundred and twenty-third viewing of *As You Like It*. Their livelihood is possibly made more safe or acceptable if a certain cultural cash flow is maintained. Otherwise, even more might begin to doubt the usefulness of their pension-rated calling.

In the case of these two particular, more accessible works, they had most certainly not gone unperformed. Indeed, there are times when Ibsen's play seems rarely out of the general repertory, constantly being seized upon by actresses who complain that the English canon contains a meagre selection of parts 'written for women'. This absurd grumble fell upon eager, rallying ears by the sort of men who like to flatter such ladies by referring reverentially to them as Ms, rather than Miss or the simple old Dame. One wonders how, if this example of a wicked male conspiracy were the case, so many female actors had managed to achieve such huge reputations. How had the likes of Mrs Siddons, Ellen Terry, Bernhardt, Duse, Dames Edith, Sybil and Peggy become so famous, loved and admired? And all in the face of such paucity of material? The range of parts written for women by men didn't seem to sustain the myth of women being systematically ignored or ill-served by playwrights during five centuries. Shakespeare (admittedly constrained by the contemporary use of boys), Congreve, Wilde, Chekhov, Shaw, Coward, to name only a smattering of the First Eleven, seemed to have provided a list of famous opportunities. This did not include the Alpine heights offered to them by the likes of Corneille and Racine, enabling them to boom mad bluster in Gallic glory for a century and a half of rapturous, male applause. For various reasons, all the lady writers with time on their hands, Jane Austen, the Brontës, George Eliot, old Auntie Virginia and their successors, seemed to reject conspicuously the public power of the stage in favour of the novel or poetry.

Now, in spite of feverish inducements and campaigning for the last twenty years, no woman playwright seems to have set us on our heels with a revivable vehicle for an actress. They are all, and continue to be, written by, yes, men. Feminism, like socialism, hasn't added much more than the merest pinch of season to the pot of world literature and least of all to drama. Hardly at all, unless you include the works of a considerable army of popular lady dramatists like Enid Bagnold, Esther McCracken, Dodie Smith, Leslie Storm, Mary Hayley Bell, Bridget Boland, Clemence Dane, Ann Jellicoe, Shelagh Delaney and, more recently, Caryl Churchill.

Some may have difficulty in remembering the parts they wrote for women. Still, they all enjoyed their support and admiration in their day. Their appeal to audiences surely disposes of partisan claims of male domination or conspiracy. Earnest liberalism, the shameless eunuch of feminism, had become so pushy and noisome around the sixties and seventies that a moratorium on further productions of, at least, *Hedda*, would have been a relief to even the most rabid enthusiast for our old friend, the Neglected Masterpiece.

The Father is altogether a different case. I read the play quickly in an eighty-year-old translation by Edgar Bjökman and N. Erichsen ('Nelly' Erichsen, an object of Shaw's several early, virginal passions). I say 'quickly', because even in this rather crusty version with its stiff Edwardian cadences, the sensation was like being pitched headlong from page to page astride an unstoppable beast of pounding dramatic energy. Once mounted, there was no question of getting off, remounting and putting the brute back on the bit. Although I was in the process of saddling up my own latest entrant for the theatrical stakes, the 'challenge', as ambitious actresses are prone to say about their latest unremarkable enterprise, was irresistible. It was more than a challenge. It seemed to me a special beholden duty to be honoured. Incorrectly or not, I was convinced that I was uniquely placed by temperament, tradition, similarities of experience and personal style to render the play into a convincing modern English version.

If anyone was to carry the Strindberg torch into the arena, I knew I was destined to be the undisputed chosen runner. I had never felt such proprietary instincts for the work of another playwright, and I was determined that if anyone were to become the keeper of that unpredictable flame, the task should be recklessly entrusted to me. I was Strindberg's Man in England. He had been done such grievous disservice in his own land and time and after, I hoped that I could make some petty reparation for his sufferings, vilification and enduring exile.

To my dismay, the casting of the National Theatre revival had already been completed. Most of the actors were unknown to me, as was the director. However, all theatrical enterprises are more or less calculated exercises in compromise and I felt that the opportunity of acting as Strindberg's guardian was not to be passed over because of my immediate practical reservations or misgivings, particularly because I knew that these were certainly coloured by my remembrance of Wilfred Lawson's legendary performance thirty-five years earlier. Like many of my generation I had been mesmerized by that occasion. Young actors and directors who had been fortunate to witness it were indelibly influenced by its hammering impact. It was to become part of the common currency of cherished theatrical memory, like the first half of Wolfit's Lear, the echoing excesses of Ernest Milton, Peggy Ashcroft's Hedda or more famous landmarks, like Olivier's Richard III. It seemed timid to be hag-ridden by the possibly esoteric shadows of past monuments. Other heroic actors had, after all, brought their undoubted powers to bear on the part, including Redgrave in 1949 and Trevor Howard in 1964.

Almost more surprising than the fact that these three productions seem to have been the only major London revivals in over forty years was that Olivier never took on this role himself, particularly while he was director of the National, when he did indeed most successfully play the lead in *Dance of Death*. It would have seemed the perfect vehicle for his own famous animal demon. Other tantalizing candidates would have been Richardson, Scofield, Finney in his prime, Denholm Elliott. And so on. You can make your own list.

Anyway, the text remains, I hope, to be restored to a regular place in the popular repertory and, no doubt, possibly improved upon by other hands. Most of all, I hope that Strindberg's reputation will be freshly valued and experienced. It is painfully susceptible to wilful and modish misinterpretation.

Firstly, there is the charge of misogyny, branded large upon his name, to which he is more than ever exposed today by tooth and claw feminism, far more insidious and virulent in its accusations than in his own time, and supported by the craven conceivings of men, themselves intimidated by the displeasure of liberal mob-ups.

Strindberg's sweeping power of humanist imagination has been adjusted to accommodate the pinched political orthodoxies of the day. This habit of political reductiveness diminishes us rather than him. His posture, and often it is a posture, and sense of rage of women manifestly exists in *The Father*, but to conceive of it as a fundamental condition is to miss the point of his prodigality and art, illuminating nothing. The ferocity of the battle between the Captain and Laura apprehends far more than an isolated account of the battle between the sexes. His constant reversion to lyricism of agonizing power, his astonishing modernism, his sense of the nineteenth century receding and, with it, the disintegration of structures of faith, moral philosophy and accepted notions of romantic love, put him, as the director of this present revival said to me, 'in the Great and Unreasonable camp of the humanists'.

Often he takes up these unremitting postures of confrontation because it was a way of getting most accurately at the heart of something in all its stark awfulness. His men strike a note of unwelcome battle which puts the fear of benighted godlessness into the ranks of the faint-hearted and pussyfooted. He gives off a shocking smell of a pervasive and longed-for notion of innocence that has been irredeemably replaced by knowledge leading to turbulence, opposition, deception and, finally, a flight to the death. A profoundly religious romantic, he wades up to his ears in opposites of almost neurasthenic proportions and makes assaults on anything and anybody who seeks to threaten his capacity for conquering the world. Such men, such poets, are not to be easily forgotten.

JOHN OSBORNE
October 1988

CHARACTERS

THE CAPTAIN
LAURA, his wife
BERTHA, their daughter
THE PASTOR
DOCTOR ÖSTERMARK
OLD MARGARET, the nurse
NÖJD

This version of *The Father* was first performed at the Cottesloe Theatre, South Bank, London, on 26 October 1988. The cast was as follows:

CAPTAIN	Alun Armstrong
PASTOR	Alan Downer
NÖJD	Stefan Escreet
LAURA	Susan Fleetwood
DOCTOR ÖSTERMARK	Colin Stinton
OLD MARGARET	Jean Heywood
BERTHA	Sarah-Jane Fenton
MAID	Laura Shavin
Directed by	David Leveaux
Designed by	Annie Smart
Lighting	Christopher Toulmin
Music	Giles Swayne

ACT ONE

A living room in the Captain's house. Tidy, masculine but not oppressively, comfortable and orderly, leather, well-used furniture, brass and mellowed wood. Maps, weapons, swords, pistols, heliographs, memorabilia, library steps, hanging weapons, cavalry and equestrian curiosities, astronomical charts, hanging greatcoats and so on.

The CAPTAIN *is in undress uniform, coaching boots and spurs. The* PASTOR *is in black with white neckerchief but without clerical collar. He is smoking a pipe. They are evidently waiting. The* CAPTAIN *takes out his pocket watch.*

CAPTAIN: Well, that bastard's been at it again. Oh – pardon.

PASTOR: Who?

CAPTAIN: Nöjd. You know.

PASTOR: Oh, yes. Nöjd. I remember. What's he been up to?

CAPTAIN: Same old thing. Sniffing up the maid again. He's hopeless.

PASTOR: I thought you said he's been doing rather well since the last little incident.

CAPTAIN: Yes, he had. Do you think you could have a go at him? A few words from you might do the trick. I've pitched into him, even belted him but nothing seems to work.

PASTOR: You want me to bring up God's own artillery? You think my guns can frighten off the cavalry?

CAPTAIN: My dear brother-in-law, they've never deterred me, as you well know.

PASTOR: Indeed.

CAPTAIN: But with the likes of him – well, perhaps at least it's worth a try.

(Enter NÖJD.*)*

Well, Nöjd, what have you been up to then?

NÖJD: No offence, Captain, but I don't think I can discuss it in front of the Pastor here.

PASTOR: My boy, you needn't be shy in front of me.

CAPTAIN: Come on, you'd better own up to it all. You know what the alternatives are.

NÖJD: All right then. There was this dance going on at Gabriel's place. And Ludwig said . . .

CAPTAIN: What's Ludwig got to do with it? Stick to the facts, boy.

NÖJD: Well, then Emma, she said, 'Why don't we go out to the barns?'

CAPTAIN: Oh, so it was Emma, was it, leading *you* astray?

NÖJD: Well, yes, I suppose she was. *You* know, sir, they always give you a pretty good idea when they *really* want it.

CAPTAIN: Oh, come along, Nöjd: are you the father of this child or not?

NÖJD: How should I know?

CAPTAIN: You mean you don't *know*?

NÖJD: No. You can't *tell*. Not for sure anyway.

CAPTAIN: You mean – you weren't the only one?

NÖJD: Well, that time yes. But you don't know who's been up there before, do you?

CAPTAIN: You mean Ludwig? You're blaming him?

NÖJD: I'm not blaming anybody.

CAPTAIN: But still you've told Emma you'll marry her.

NÖJD: You've got to, haven't you?

CAPTAIN: (*To* PASTOR) A right mess!

PASTOR: A pretty familiar one. Nöjd. Surely you're enough of a man to know whether or not you're the father?

NÖJD: Well, I was in there all right. But you know as well as me, Pastor, that needn't signify necessarily with later developments.

PASTOR: Listen, lad, it's you we're talking about, here and now. Surely you don't want to leave this girl, on her own, with a child? You can't be forced to marry her, I suppose. But you'll jolly well provide for the child, take it from me.

NÖJD: Well, all right, but Ludwig has to help as well.

CAPTAIN: That'll be for the courts to decide. I can't do any more. It's nothing to do with me. All right, clear off out!

PASTOR: Hang on, Nöjd. Don't you think it's a bit vile, leaving a girl like that, penniless with a baby? Don't you think so? Come on, answer me! Don't you think that kind of carrying on is just, well, a bit . . .

NÖJD: Yes, I do. If I knew for certain I was the child's father. But I don't, Pastor. You never *can* know. And working your arse off all your life to keep another man's kid is no joke. You must see that. (*To* CAPTAIN) *You* do, don't you, Captain? *You* do.

CAPTAIN: Clear off!

(NÖJD *goes*.)

And keep out of the kitchen, you bastard! (*To* PASTOR) Well, why didn't you let him have it?

PASTOR: I thought I did.

CAPTAIN: Mumble, jumble . . .

PASTOR: Quite honestly, I wasn't really sure what to say. It's tough luck on the girl, I agree, but so it is on him. As he says, suppose he's *not* the father? All the girl's got to do is stay in the orphanage for four months, nurse the child and then she's off the hook for the rest of its life. The boy doesn't even get those first few months. When the time's up, the girl can always get a good job with a decent family. But the boy, he's left facing dismissal from his regiment, total ruination.

CAPTAIN: My God, yes. I wouldn't like the judge's job like this. Who'd ever know for sure whether the lad's guilty or not? But her – she must be guilty – if there is such a thing . . .

PASTOR: Well then, who am I . . . Where were we before all this? Oh yes, Bertha – her confirmation . . .

CAPTAIN: Not just her confirmation. Her whole upbringing. This house is filled with women, all intent on raising my daughter. My mother-in-law wants to turn her into some table-rapping loon. Laura, my wife, she thinks she's some kind of artist. The governess wants to make a Methodist of her. Old Margaret insists she's a Baptist and the maids, they want her banging the drum for the Salvation Army. You can't put someone like that together, from the outside. Most particularly, there's myself, *I* should have the final voice, and all I get is

opposition. I tell you, I've got to get her away from
here.

PASTOR: You do have a lot of women running things for you.

CAPTAIN: You don't need to tell me. It's like living in a cage
full of tigers: if I didn't keep a red-hot poker under their
noses they'd tear me apart. Oh, you may laugh, you
devil. It's bad enough being married to your own little
sister, you've even dumped your old stepmother on me
to boot.

PASTOR: Good heavens, I don't see why a man can't put up
with a stepmother in the house.

CAPTAIN: Oh yes – a mother-in-law, that's fine. For you. As
long as it's in somone else's house.

PASTOR: We all have our cross . . .

CAPTAIN: To bear, oh yes. Who bears it? I do. I'm even
lumbered with my old nurse, treating me as if I'm still
in nappies. She's a darling old thing, but she's no
business being here.

PASTOR: You should keep your womenfolk in control,
Captain. You let them make rings round you.

CAPTAIN: Very well, then, you tell me how to manage them.

PASTOR: Laura was always, well, wilful and obstinate. She's
my own sister but she can be very tedious indeed.

CAPTAIN: Laura's got her faults. But they're not
insurmountable.

PASTOR: Go on – say what you think. I do know her.

CAPTAIN: She's been brought up on too many starry clouds.
She doesn't know where she is or what she's at, etc.
However, she's still my wife . . .

PASTOR: And because she is your wife, she's got to be the
best. No, my friend, she is the one, she is your trouble.

CAPTAIN: Anyhow, the entire household is in turmoil. Laura
won't let go of Bertha and I can't let her go on staying in
this madhouse.

PASTOR: Laura won't let go. Oh dear, well then you are in
trouble. When she was a child she'd lie on the floor
pretending to be dead until she got her way. Then,
when she did, she'd give back whatever it was and say it

wasn't any . . . *thing* she wanted. Only her precious
way.

CAPTAIN: So, she was always the same . . . Sometimes she is
in such a state of rage, I think she must be quite ill. It
frightens me.

PASTOR: What is it about your plans for Bertha that stirs all
this up? Is there no compromise somewhere?

CAPTAIN: Don't think I want to make her into some prodigy
– not even another version of myself. I won't become
just a marriage broker for my daughter with nothing in
her head but damned wedding bells. What if she should
never marry at all? Would that be so terrible? On the
other hand, I don't want to shackle her to some long,
arduous training and career that she'll only give up for
some dream of marriage when it comes along.

PASTOR: What *do* you want?

CAPTAIN: I want her to be a teacher. Then, if she doesn't
marry, she can always support herself. She certainly
wouldn't be as badly off as those schoolmasters on a
teacher's pittance and burdened with a squalling family
of ever open-mouthed cuckoos. If she does choose to get
married, she can use her gifts and learning on caring for
her own brood. Aren't I right?

PASTOR: You are. But what about her painting? If Laura is
right about her talent, as she may be, it would be cruel
surely to override *that*.

CAPTAIN: Not a bit of it. I showed some of her work to a
painter friend of mine. Someone who knows the real
thing all right. He said it was charming, very pleasing,
pleasing schoolgirl stuff. No more than that . . . Then,
of course, last summer along comes some little upstart
faker, Mr Arty Knowall, he tells Laura we've got it all
wrong. Our Bertha's a genius. And that was it as far as
Laura's concerned.

PASTOR: He's fallen for the girl, I suppose?

CAPTAIN: What else!

PASTOR: Well, may God help you, my dear boy, because I
can't see much help coming for you from anywhere else.
It's a very sad business for you. And then, of course,

Laura does have her allies – (*points to door*) through there . . .

CAPTAIN: She has indeed. The whole house is in ferment. Between you and me, they're none too picky about the kind of weapons they handle.

(*The* PASTOR *rises.*)

PASTOR: You think I don't know?

CAPTAIN: You as well.

PASTOR: Oh, yes.

CAPTAIN: The worst of it is, they've already made up their minds about Bertha's future and they've done it out of hatred. They witter on about men being forced to tell that women can do this, women can do that, women can do God knows what. It's man versus woman all day long in this house, unremitting, unending, unrelenting. My dear chap, you aren't going? Please, do stay for supper. It won't be anything much, but don't go. Oh yes, and I'm expecting the new doctor to come round. Have you met him?

PASTOR: I caught a glimpse of him on the way here. He looked quite a decent sort.

CAPTAIN: Did he? Do you think he might be an ally? For *me*, that is?

PASTOR: It could be. It depends on how much time he's spent amongst women.

CAPTAIN: Please, won't you stay?

PASTOR: I'm afraid I really can't. I promised to be home for supper, and the old lady gets upset if I'm late.

CAPTAIN: Upset? Furious, you mean. Well, it's up to you. Let me give you a hand.

(*Helps the* PASTOR *into his coat.*)

PASTOR: It's suddenly turned very cold. Yes, thank you. Do have a care for yourself, Captain. You seem a bit of a riderless horse at the moment.

CAPTAIN: I do?

PASTOR: Yes. Are you quite well?

CAPTAIN: Oh, Laura's put that into your head. She's been perching over my deathbed for twenty years.

PASTOR: No. It wasn't Laura. It's worrying to see you the
way you are. So take care of yourself, that's all.
Goodbye, old man. Oh – we still haven't decided about
her confirmation.

CAPTAIN: It doesn't matter. That can go ahead in the
ordinary way. I leave the detail to you. I'm no witness to
the faith and no martyr either. We've gone over all that
too many times. Goodnight. Remember me to everyone.

PASTOR: Goodnight, my friend. And to Laura, of course.

CAPTAIN: Laura. Of course.

(*The* PASTOR *goes. The* CAPTAIN *opens the desk and sits
down to his accounting.*)

Thirty-four – nine – fifty-three – seven, eight, fifty-six.

(LAURA *enters.*)

LAURA: Would you mind, please . . .

CAPTAIN: Just a minute. Sixty-six, seventy-one, eighty-four,
eighty-nine, ninety-two, a hundred. Yes, what is it?

LAURA: Am I interrupting?

CAPTAIN: Not at all. I suppose you want the housekeeping.

LAURA: Yes, the housekeeping money.

CAPTAIN: Leave the accounts there, and I'll go over them.

LAURA: Accounts?

CAPTAIN: That's right.

LAURA: You mean I have to keep accounts now?

CAPTAIN: Of course you must keep accounts. Our affairs are
in an absolute mess, and if I do go bust, I've got to be
able to produce accounts. Otherwise I'll be told I'm
negligent.

LAURA: It's not my fault if you're going bust as you call it.

CAPTAIN: Then I'm sure the accounts will agree with you.

LAURA: I can't help it if your tenants won't cough up.

CAPTAIN: And who was it was so damned keen on the
tenant? You! You were the one all for this dumb-headed
waster.

LAURA: If you thought he was such a dumb-headed waster,
why did you take him on?

CAPTAIN: Because: because I wasn't allowed to eat, sleep or
work in peace until you'd got him in here. And *you*
wanted him because your brother wanted to get rid of

7

him. Your mother wanted him because I *didn't* want
him. The governess wanted him because he was a
Pietist. And Old Margaret, she wanted him because
she's known his grandmother since childhood. That's
why I took him on. Because if I hadn't I would either be
in the lunatic asylum by now or the family vault.
Notwithstanding that, here is the housekeeping money
and there is your allowance. You can give me the
accounts later.

(LAURA *drops a curtsy.*)

LAURA: Thank you so much! And you – I suppose you keep
accounts of everything you spend – apart from the
housekeeping?

CAPTAIN: That's none of your business.

LAURA: That's right – just as my child's education is none of
my business. So, did you gentlemen come to any
decision at tonight's little conference?

CAPTAIN: My decision was made already. I simply wanted to
let our mutual friend know what it was. Bertha is taking
a room in town. She leaves in a fortnight.

LAURA: May I ask where this room's to be?

CAPTAIN: With Mr Sävberg!

LAURA: Sävberg! That legal freethinker!

CAPTAIN: Children should be brought up in their father's
faith. That is the law.

LAURA: And the mother has no say in the matter?

CAPTAIN: None whatever. She surrenders all her rights and
possessions to her husband. In return he must agree to
support her and her children.

LAURA: So I have no rights over my own child?

CAPTAIN: None. Once you've sold your goods, you can't
expect to have them back *and* keep the money.

LAURA: But suppose. The father and mother agree to a
compromise?

CAPTAIN: What compromise? I want her to live in town, you
want her to live at home. To be exact, a compromise
would have to mean living halfway between the two.
What do you have in mind? The railway station? Don't
you see? There's no meeting ground in this.

8

LAURA: Then we must find one. What was Nöjd doing here?

CAPTAIN: Confidential business.

LAURA: Which only the whole kitchen knows about!

CAPTAIN: Good. Then you know as well.

LAURA: Of course I do.

CAPTAIN: No doubt you've reached your verdict.

LAURA: The law is absolutely clear.

CAPTAIN: It can't know who is the child's father.

LAURA: One knows these things.

CAPTAIN: The highest authorities don't appear to agree with you.

LAURA: Oh, that's rich. You can't be certain who a child's father is?

CAPTAIN: So it seems.

LAURA: Isn't it a little bizarre? How is it then that the father has such rights over the woman's children?

CAPTAIN: Simply because he assumes, or is forced to assume, all the responsibilities. As for doubts about paternity – in marriage – there aren't any.

LAURA: No doubts at all?

CAPTAIN: I should hope not.

LAURA: Supposing the wife were unfaithful?

CAPTAIN: That question doesn't arise here. Have you anything else to ask?

LAURA: No. Nothing.

CAPTAIN: Well, I shall go to my room. Please let me know when the doctor arrives.

(He closes the desk and gets up.)

LAURA: Just as you say.

CAPTAIN: *(As he leaves)* Just as soon as he gets here. I shouldn't like to seem rude.

(Exit.)

LAURA: I'm sure.

(She looks at the banknotes in her hand. Her MOTHER calls, off.)

MOTHER: Laura!

LAURA: Yes!

MOTHER: Is my tea ready?

LAURA: Just coming.

(DOCTOR ÖSTERMARK *enters*.)

Oh!

DOCTOR: Good evening, madam.

LAURA: Good evening.

DOCTOR: Östermark.

LAURA: Doctor Östermark. Of course. Please come in. The Captain is out but he won't be long.

DOCTOR: I'm sorry to be so late but I had to look in on some patients on the way.

LAURA: Do sit down, Doctor.

DOCTOR: Thank you.

LAURA: Yes, there's a lot of illness around lately but I'm sure you'll cope with that. It can be very lonely here in the country. So having a doctor who's really interested in his patients means a great deal. I've heard so many nice things about you, Doctor. I've a feeling we'll get on really well together.

DOCTOR: You're very kind. For your sake though I hope my *professional* visits won't be very often. I should imagine your family keeps pretty healthy and –

LAURA: We've been lucky to escape anything serious. All the same, things aren't exactly quite normal.

DOCTOR: Really?

LAURA: No. In fact, there's room for a great deal of improvement.

DOCTOR: That's rather disturbing.

LAURA: There are certain things, things within the family that loyalty and, yes, love demand one to keep secure from the world outside.

DOCTOR: But not from one's doctor.

LAURA: That's why it's my duty, painful as I find it, to tell you the whole truth from the beginning.

DOCTOR: Don't you think it might perhaps be better to wait until I've had the pleasure of meeting the Captain?

LAURA: No. You have to hear me out first.

DOCTOR: I take it this is really about him?

LAURA: Yes. It's him – my poor, dearest husband.

DOCTOR: I'm sorry to hear this from you, madam. I only hope I can be helpful.

LAURA: (LAURA *takes out her handkerchief*.) My husband is
        deranged. It's his mind. Well, now you know. You'll see
        what I mean when you see him for yourself.
DOCTOR: It's a little difficult to believe. I have actually read
        some of the Captain's amazing work on mineralogy.
        They seemed, to me at least, the evidence of an
        especially authoritative and, well, lucid mind.
LAURA: Did they? Well, it would make all those who are
        nearest to him very happy to be proved wrong.
DOCTOR: Tell me more. It could be that his mind is affected
        in some way that no one has yet examined.
LAURA: That's what we're all afraid of. You see, he
        sometimes suffers from the most outlandish notions. Of
        course that's not unusual in certain brilliant men. It's
        even acceptable but not, not when those notions threaten
        the very heart of his whole family. I'll give you an
        example: he has a mania for buying things.
DOCTOR: That could be enlightening. What sort of things
        does he buy?
LAURA: Great stacks of books. None of which he ever reads.
DOCTOR: For a scholar to buy books isn't very odd.
LAURA: Don't you believe what I'm saying to you?
DOCTOR: Madam, I'm quite sure that *you* believe what you're
        telling me.
LAURA: Tell me: would you say that it was reasonable for a
        man to see what's happening on another planet –
        through a microscope?
DOCTOR: Is that what he claims to do?
LAURA: He does.
DOCTOR: Through a microscope?
LAURA: Yes. Through a microscope.
DOCTOR: Well, that's instructive – if it's true.
LAURA: If it's true! So you won't believe me. And there I've
        been opening our family secret to you . . .
DOCTOR: My dear lady, please. I'm honoured that you
        should trust in me. But, as a doctor, I have to examine,
        pursue, confirm before I make any conclusions. Does
        the Captain ever show signs of erratic behaviour? Fits of
        unpredictability?

LAURA: Unpredictable? We've been married for twenty years and he's never made a decision yet and not changed it.

DOCTOR: Is he stubborn?

LAURA: He always has to have his own way. Then, when he gets it, he ducks out of it, and *I* have to decide for him.

DOCTOR: It does seem to add together. Anyway, it should be looked into. You see, madam, the will is the spinal cord of the spirit. If it should be damaged, the personality, the whole inner life is broken.

LAURA: God knows, I've gone along with him all these long, exhausting years. Oh, if only you knew what I've endured, bound and tied to *him*, if you had any *idea*!

DOCTOR: Madam, believe me, this account of your difficulties is indeed, well, disturbing. And I promise you I'll do whatever I can. I sympathize with you absolutely and I hope you will trust me. However, from what you've told me, I must impress on you one thing. Don't bring up anything that might disturb him any further. Any random fancy put into a patient's head can lead into almost anything – obsessions, fantasies, self-aggrandizements of every kind. Do you understand?

LAURA: You mean, don't feed his suspicions?

DOCTOR: That's right. Patients like these can be induced to believe anything. Just because they are so susceptible.

LAURA: Yes. I understand that. Yes. Yes.

(*A bell rings from inside.*)

Please excuse me. My mother wants me for something. I'll just be a moment. – Ah, the Captain. He's here.

(*The* CAPTAIN *enters.*)

CAPTAIN: Ah, Doctor, you're here already. We're delighted to have you here.

DOCTOR: My dear Captain, it's indeed an honour to come face to face with such a distinguished man of science.

CAPTAIN: Please! My military commitments leave me no time for serious research. Even so, I do believe I'm on the threshold of a vital breakthrough.

DOCTOR: Is that so?

CAPTAIN: It's like this: I've made exhaustive spectral analysis

12

tests on meteoric material. And what do you think I found? I found *coal* – in other words, organic life. What about that?

DOCTOR: And you saw that through a microscope?

CAPTAIN: Good God, no – through a spectroscope.

DOCTOR: A spectroscope! Yes, of course, forgive me. So soon you'll be able to tell us what's going on in Jupiter?

CAPTAIN: Not what is happening but what *has* happened. If only those damned booksellers in Paris would send me the books I've asked for. Sometimes I think all the world's booksellers must be conspiring against me. For two whole months, would you believe it, not one has acknowledged a single order. Not a letter, even when I've sent abusive telegrams. It's driving me mad. I can't think what they're up to.

DOCTOR: Oh, it's probably just bloody-minded negligence. I shouldn't let it get you down.

CAPTAIN: If it goes on like this, I'll never get my thesis finished in time. And I know in Berlin they're already on to it. Still, we're not here to talk about that. Now what about yourself? If you feel like staying here, there's a small flat in the annexe. Or perhaps you'd prefer the doctor's old quarters?

DOCTOR: I leave it to you.

CAPTAIN: No, it's up to you. You say.

DOCTOR: I'd like *you* to decide, Captain.

CAPTAIN: I'm not making decisions. You must tell me what you want. It's all the same to me. I've no prejudice, preferences or opinions. You must know your own mind. What sort of a waffler are you? Now, do cast your vote or I may be losing my patience.

DOCTOR: In that case: I prefer to stay here.

CAPTAIN: Right then. That's a relief. Forgive me, Doctor, but nothing irks me more than indecision.

(*He rings the bell and the* NURSE *enters.*)

Ah, this is Margaret, my old nurse. Listen, my old dear, do you know if the annexe is ready for the doctor?

NURSE: Yes, Captain. It's all prepared.

CAPTAIN: Splendid. Well, I shan't keep you, Doctor.

I expect you're tired. Goodbye then. I look forward to seeing you in the morning.

DOCTOR: Goodnight, Captain.

CAPTAIN: I dare say my wife's filled you in about our little household ways, so you'll have some idea about the way things are run.

DOCTOR: Your charming wife has given me a kind of handy visitor's guide.

CAPTAIN: Fine, fine.

DOCTOR: Goodnight again, Captain.

(*He goes.*)

CAPTAIN: (*To* NURSE) What do you want, my old dear?

NURSE: Now, young master, just you listen to me.

CAPTAIN: What is it, old girl? Let's have it. You're the only woman I can listen to without going barmy.

NURSE: Do try and listen to me, sir. Don't you think you could meet your wife halfway over this business of the child? Can't you and madam be friends again? You must be sensitive to a mother's feelings –

CAPTAIN: And what about a father's feelings, Margaret? What about those?

NURSE: Now then, now then. A father has other things to occupy him. A mother has only her child.

CAPTAIN: There you have it, my old dear. She has one burden only. I have three and hers thrown in on top of the lot. If I hadn't had all that to bear, don't you think I might have ended up something more than an old soldier?

NURSE: That's not what I meant.

CAPTAIN: No, I'm sure. You wanted me to admit to being in the wrong.

NURSE: My dear, don't you think I want to be your help?

CAPTAIN: Yes, old friend, I do indeed but you don't happen to know what's best for me. You see, it isn't enough for me just to have given the child life. I want her to have my *self*.

NURSE: Oh, I don't know about all that. I still think you can both find some way round.

CAPTAIN: You're not being a friend, Margaret.

14

NURSE: Me. Oh, Master Adolf, what are you thinking of? Do you think I could ever forget you were my own little baby?

CAPTAIN: Do you think I could forget it either? You've been a mother to me. When everyone's been against me, you've always taken my side. Until now. But now, now when I really need you, you turn against me and go over to the enemy.

NURSE: The enemy?

CAPTAIN: Yes, the enemy! You know full well how things stand in this household. You've witnessed it all, from beginning to end.

NURSE: Oh, I've witnessed it all right. But, good God, why should two people plague each other to death? Two people who are so kind and good to others. Madam is never like this with me or anyone else.

CAPTAIN: Only to me – I know. I tell you, Margaret: if you abandon me now, you'll be doing me a terrible evil. It would be criminal and a sin. They're spinning a web around me. And as for that doctor – he's no friend of mine either.

NURSE: Come along, sir. You do think the worst of everyone. And why's that? I'll tell you why. You don't have the true faith, that's why.

CAPTAIN: And you and your Baptists do have the true faith. You're a happy little lot, aren't you?

NURSE: Not unhappy as you are, sir. Bow down your heart humbly. God will receive it from you and make you happy and loving towards your neighbours.

CAPTAIN: It's a funny thing but every time you talk about God and love, your voice becomes hard and your eyes fill with hatred. No, Margaret, you don't have the true faith.

NURSE: All that knowledge of yours may make you proud and hard, but that won't get you very far in the end.

CAPTAIN: If yours is a humble heart, it sounds pretty proud from here. Oh, I know how little my strivings for discovery mean to your kind.

NURSE: You should be ashamed to be so high and mighty.

Still, whatever wild things you may say, your old
Margaret always loves her great, big boy the best. And
when he's in trouble, he'll come rushing back to her
again first, just like the dear little boy he used to be.

CAPTAIN: I'm sorry, Margaret. But take it from me, you're
the only one in this house I can look to. You've got to
help me. Because I know full well that something's
going to happen here. I don't know what it'll be, but
whatever it is, it will be something evil.

(*Scream off.*)

Who's that? Who screamed?

(BERTHA *comes in.*)

BERTHA: Papa, help. Save me, Papa. Help!

CAPTAIN: My darling child! What is it? Tell me.

BERTHA: You've got to help me. She wants to hurt me. She
really does, she wants to.

CAPTAIN: Who's trying to hurt you? Now tell me who it is.

BERTHA: Grandmama. Grandmama does. It was my own
fault. I played her along.

CAPTAIN: What did you do? Go on, then.

BERTHA: All right, but you mustn't tell anyone. You won't,
will you? Please say you won't.

CAPTAIN: Just tell me what it's all about.

(*Exit* NURSE.)

BERTHA: Well, sometimes in the evenings, she turns down
all the lights and then she makes me sit down at the
table and hold a pen over a sheet of paper. And then,
then she summons up the spirits to write.

CAPTAIN: What are you telling me? You've never mentioned
this before.

BERTHA: I'm sorry but I didn't dare. Grandmama says the
spirits take their revenge if you betray them. And then
the pen writes but I don't know if it's me doing it or
not. Sometimes it works wonderfully and then
sometimes it doesn't work at all. When I'm tired it
doesn't write but I have to make something happen.
This evening I thought I was doing it really well but
Grandmama said it was all a pack of tricks and that I'd
been making fun of her and she got terribly angry.

16

CAPTAIN: You mean you actually believe in spirits?

BERTHA: I don't know.

CAPTAIN: Well, I do. And they don't exist.

BERTHA: But Grandmama says you don't understand and that, anyway, you have things that are far worse, things that see what goes on in other planets.

CAPTAIN: She says that, does she? What else does she say?

BERTHA: She says you can't do magic.

CAPTAIN: I never said I could. You know what meteors are? They're lumps of rock that fall from other heavenly bodies. All I do is examine them to find out whether they contain the same elements as earth. That's all I can see.

BERTHA: But she says, Grandmama says, that she can see things you can't.

CAPTAIN: Then she's lying.

BERTHA: Grandmama doesn't lie.

CAPTAIN: Why not?

BERTHA: In that case, Mama is a liar too.

CAPTAIN: Well –

BERTHA: If you say that Mama tells lies I'll never believe you again.

CAPTAIN: I didn't say that. And that's why you've got to believe me when I tell you that you've got to leave home. It's for your own good. And the good of your whole future. You have to leave this house. Now will you do that? Wouldn't you like to live in town and learn something of proper use to you?

BERTHA: Oh, yes! I long to move out to the town – anywhere to get out of here. As long as I can see you sometimes – often. Oh, it's always so miserable and dull in there – like some dreadful winter night. But when you come, Papa, it's like the spring morning when the shutters have come down.

CAPTAIN: My darling heart!

BERTHA: But, you must promise to be kind to Mama. Promise me, Papa. She cries so bitterly.

CAPTAIN: Does she? So you want to move out?

BERTHA: Oh, please, yes!

CAPTAIN: But suppose Mama doesn't wish it?

BERTHA: Oh, she must.

CAPTAIN: What if she doesn't?

BERTHA: Then I don't know what will happen. But she's got to, she must. She'll want me to, I know she will.

CAPTAIN: Will you ask her?

BERTHA: No, you ask her – really nicely. She'll never listen to me.

CAPTAIN: Hm. Well, suppose it's what you want and what I want, but she doesn't. What happens then?

BERTHA: Oh, everything will be vile again. Why can't the two of you . . .

(LAURA *enters.*)

LAURA: Ah, so this is where Bertha's got to. Then perhaps we can hear *her* opinion, seeing it's *her* future that's being decided.

CAPTAIN: The child can hardly have any mature opinion about the course a young girl's life may take. You and I, on the other hand, have watched plenty of girls growing up, so it should be rather easier for us to work out some reasonable solution for her.

LAURA: Since our ideas are utterly different, why don't we let Bertha make up her own mind?

CAPTAIN: No! I'll not have anyone – girl or woman – poaching on my rights. Bertha, go outside.

(BERTHA *goes.*)

LAURA: You were afraid to let her answer because you knew she'd side with me.

CAPTAIN: I do know that she wants to leave home. I also know that you've got the power to make her change her mind whenever you like.

LAURA: Oh, I'm so powerful, am I?

CAPTAIN: Yes, when it comes to getting your own way, you've got some kind of satanic gift. So has anyone who doesn't give a damn for scruples. For instance, how was it you got rid of Dr Nordling and got this new one in?

LAURA: I wonder. How did I do that?

CAPTAIN: You insulted Nordling so that he left and then you

recruited your brother to whistle up the votes for this
one.

LAURA: Well, it wasn't very difficult and quite above board.
So, Bertha's going then?

CAPTAIN: Yes. She leaves in a fortnight.

LAURA: And that's what you've decided?

CAPTAIN: It is.

LAURA: Have you told Bertha?

CAPTAIN: Yes.

LAURA: Then it's up to me to stop it.

CAPTAIN: You can't.

LAURA: Oh, no? Do you really think a mother can be willed
into letting her child out among wicked people who'll
tell her that everything her mother has taught her is
rubbish? Any daughter would end up despising her for
ever.

CAPTAIN: And do you think that any father would allow a
bunch of ignorant and conceited women to teach his
daughter that he's a charlatan?

LAURA: It isn't so important to a father.

CAPTAIN: It isn't. And why?

LAURA: Because a mother is closer to a child's heart. It's
common knowledge that no one, no one can ever truly
know for certain who is a child's father.

CAPTAIN: What has that to do with us?

LAURA: Only that you cannot know whether or not you are
Bertha's father.

CAPTAIN: Of course I know.

LAURA: You can't know. Neither can anyone.

CAPTAIN: Is this some joke?

LAURA: No. I'm simply following your own doctrine.
Besides, how do you know that I haven't been unfaithful
to you?

CAPTAIN: I can believe a lot of things about you, but that's
not one of them. And if it were true I'm certain you'd
never own up to it.

LAURA: Well, think on this: what if I were prepared to put
up with anything, humiliation, losing my reputation, my

19

home, anything for the sake of holding on to my child and bringing her up? What if I were just telling the truth when I said Bertha was my child and not yours? Suppose –

CAPTAIN: Stop it!

LAURA: Bite on that! Where would your rights be then?

CAPTAIN: You'd have to prove I was not the father!

LAURA: That wouldn't be so difficult. Would you like me to?

CAPTAIN: Stop it!

LAURA: All I have to do is give the name of the real father, details of the time, the place. For instance – when was Bertha born? Three years after we'd been married –

CAPTAIN: That's enough! Otherwise, I'll –

LAURA: Otherwise, you'll what? All right then. We'll leave it there. But think very carefully before you decide anything. And above all, don't make yourself look ridiculous.

CAPTAIN: I find this very distasteful.

LAURA: That makes you even more ridiculous.

CAPTAIN: But not you?

LAURA: No. We women are a little cleverer in the way we manage these things.

CAPTAIN: That's why we can't fight you.

LAURA: Then why take on a superior enemy?

CAPTAIN: Superior?

LAURA: Yes. It's odd. I've never been able to look at a man without feeling superior.

CAPTAIN: Well, one day you'll find your match. Face to face. And you'll never forget it!

LAURA: That should be interesting.

(NURSE enters.)

NURSE: Supper's on the table. Are you ready?

LAURA: Yes. I'm ready.

(The CAPTAIN slumps.)

Aren't you coming in to supper?

CAPTAIN: No, thank you. I don't want anything.

LAURA: Oh? There's nothing wrong, is there?

CAPTAIN: No. I'm not hungry.

LAURA: Oh, come along, Captain. Otherwise people will start

asking silly questions. Please. No? Very well. If you
won't, don't.

(LAURA *goes*.)

NURSE: Oh, Master Adolf. What is wrong?

CAPTAIN: I don't know. Can you explain to me how it is that
you women manage to deal with a grown man as if he
were a small child?

NURSE: I couldn't say. Maybe it's because you are all
women's children, every born man of you, great ones or
small ones . . .

CAPTAIN: And no woman ever came forth from a man. But I
am still Bertha's father. Margaret, please, you do believe
that, don't you?

NURSE: Dear God, what a little child you are. Of course
you're the father of your own child. Come along and get
your supper now and don't sit there and brood. There!
Come on now!

(*The* CAPTAIN *rises*.)

CAPTAIN: Get out, woman! Go to hell, all you witches. (*To
the door*) Hey, you out there. Someone harness up the
sleigh for me! Come on, somebody. Harness up!

NURSE: Captain, please listen to me.

CAPTAIN: Get out, woman! Out! Now!

NURSE: God save us! What's happening to us?

(*The* CAPTAIN *puts on his cap, preparing to leave*.)

CAPTAIN: Don't expect me home before midnight.

(*Exit*.)

NURSE: Oh, Jesus, help! What will become of us?

(*Curtain*.)

ACT TWO

The same as the previous act. Night time. The light on the table is alight.
The DOCTOR *and* LAURA.

DOCTOR: Even accepting everything that you have told me, I still cannot feel that the case against the Captain is convincingly made out. To begin with, you were quite wrong about his remarkable discoveries among the other planets. You told me that these were made with the use of a microscope. Unsurprisingly, it turns out to have been a spectroscope, which not only dispels any misgivings about his sanity, but confirms his startling scientific originality.

LAURA: But I never said that.

DOCTOR: Madam, I made a note of our conversation and I remember putting that specific point to you because I thought I must have misheard you. One has to be meticulous about making accusations that could lead a man to be certified.

LAURA: Certified?

DOCTOR: Of course. You must know that someone certified as insane is deprived of all his civil and family rights?

LAURA: I didn't realize that.

DOCTOR: Then there's another point that strikes me as suspect. He mentioned his correspondence with the booksellers going unanswered. Forgive me, but I must ask you: was that correspondence, perhaps out of misplaced concern, intercepted by you?

LAURA: Yes. I did intercept it. It was my duty to protect the interests of the house. I couldn't stand by and let him ruin us all.

DOCTOR: I'm sorry, but I don't think you can have understood the consequences of your behaviour. If he were to find out that you've been secretly tampering in his affairs, he'd have all grounds for an avalanche of suspicions. What's more, you've defied his will and pitched him headlong into an abyss of unreason and

22

chaos. You must know, yourself, the turmoil of having your dearest intentions thwarted and your will undermined.

LAURA: I know that well enough.

DOCTOR: Then imagine what he's been going through.
(LAURA *rises*.)

LAURA: It's midnight, and he's not home yet. I'm certain something dreadful's happened.

DOCTOR: Tell me, what happened after I left you this evening? I've got to know everything.

LAURA: He began wandering and then this wild notion took over him. He suddenly had the idea that he wasn't the father of his own child.

DOCTOR: That's strange. How did that get into his head?

LAURA: How should I know? Maybe he had to cross-examine one of the men over a question of maintenance. Then, when I tried to support the girl, he got furious and said no one could tell with certainty who might be the father of a child. God knows I did everything I could to calm him down. Now I'm beginning to feel there's no helping him.
(*She cries.*)

DOCTOR: This can't go on. Something must be done and without making him suspicious. Tell me, has the Captain had these fits of fancy before?

LAURA: Six years ago something similar came up. Then he even owned up himself in a letter to the doctor that he was – in fear of his mind.

DOCTOR: There you are. This sort of case has the deepest roots, tangling with the sanctity of family life and who knows what. There's such a thing as digging too deeply. I have to concentrate on what's tangible. What's done is done, I'm afraid. Attention must be confined to the facts as we know them. Where do you think he's got to?

LAURA: I've no idea. There's no way of knowing what kind of fancy he'll suddenly fetch up.

DOCTOR: Do you want me to wait up with you until he gets back? To avoid suspicion I can say that your mother was unwell and I'd come to see her.

23

LAURA: Yes, tell him that. Only don't leave us, Doctor. You don't know how frantic I am. But wouldn't it be better to tell him what you think about the state he's in?

DOCTOR: That's the last way to approach someone in his condition, unless, of course, he should bring it up himself. Even then the risk is considerable. Everything depends upon the course his seizure takes. But we mustn't sit here. It might look better if I went off into the next room.

LAURA: Yes, it won't look so prepared. Then Margaret can sit here. She always waits up until he comes home. Also, she's the only one who's any power over him. (*Calling through the door*) Margaret! Margaret!

NURSE: What is it, madam? Is the master come back?

LAURA: No, but I want you to sit here and wait for him. And when he does return, you're to tell him that my mother's ill, which is the reason the doctor's here.

NURSE: Yes, yes, you just leave it to me.

LAURA: (*Opening door*) Will you come through here, Doctor?

DOCTOR: Thank you, madam.

(*The* NURSE *sits at the table, takes out her spectacles and peruses a hymn book.*)

NURSE: Yes, yes.

(*She reads quickly.*)

Come on, my partners in distress,
My comrades through the wilderness,
Who still your bodies feel;
A while forget your griefs and fears,
And look beyond this vale of tears
To that celestial hill.

Yes, yes.

Beyond the bounds of time and space,
Look forward to that heavenly place,
The saints' secure abode . . .
It lifts the fainting spirits up
It brings to life the dead . . .
Our conflicts here shall soon be past
And you and I ascend at last.

True, it's true . . .

24

(BERTHA *enters with a coffee pot and some embroidery*.)

BERTHA: (*Softly*) Margaret, may I sit with you? It's so lonely up there.

NURSE: Why, Bertha, good heavens me, aren't you in bed yet?

BERTHA: Well, I wanted to finish off Papa's Christmas present. And I've got something nice for you as well.

NURSE: Oh dear, this won't do at all. Way past midnight and you've got to be up in the morning.

BERTHA: It can't matter. I daren't stay up there alone. I think it's haunted.

NURSE: There now, what did I tell you! This house has a curse on it. What did you hear?

BERTHA: Someone was singing – in the attic. I heard it.

NURSE: In the attic? At this time of night?

BERTHA: Yes. It was such a pitiful sound, the saddest song I've ever heard. It seemed to come from that little, empty room. The one on the left, you know, where the cradle lies.

NURSE: Dear, oh dear, oh dear. And such a dreadful night. Those chimneys'll be down before it's out.

And time a maniac scattering dust
And life a fury slinging flame.

Yes, dear child, may God grant us a happy Christmas.

BERTHA: Margaret, is it true that Papa is ill?

NURSE: Yes, he is, truly.

BERTHA: Then how can we keep Christmas? But if he's ill, why is he up?

NURSE: You see, child, his kind of illness doesn't mean having to stay in bed. Quiet now, there's someone in the hall. Get off to bed and take that coffee pot or the master'll be angry.

BERTHA: (*Taking the tray*) Goodnight, Margaret.

NURSE: Goodnight, my child, and God bless you.

(The CAPTAIN *enters, removing his greatcoat*.)

CAPTAIN: Are you still up? Go to bed!

NURSE: I was only staying until –

(*The* CAPTAIN *lights a candle, opens the desk and, sitting by it, takes letters and newspapers from his pocket*.)

Mr Adolf.

CAPTAIN: What is it?

NURSE: The old lady's been taken ill and the doctor's come.

CAPTAIN: Is it serious?

NURSE: No, I don't think so. Just a cold.

(*The* CAPTAIN *gets up*.)

CAPTAIN: Margaret, who was the father of your child?

NURSE: Oh, I've told you enough times. It was that devil Johansson.

CAPTAIN: Are you sure it was him?

NURSE: Stop being so childish. Of course I'm sure. On account of he was the only one.

CAPTAIN: Yes, but was *he* sure he was the only one? No, how could he be, but you, you could be sure. And there's the difference.

NURSE: I don't see the difference.

CAPTAIN: No, you can't see it, but the difference is *there*, indisputable.

(*He flicks through a photograph album on the table*.)

Do you think Bertha's like me?

(*He looks at a photograph in the album*.)

NURSE: I should say so. Alike as two peas.

CAPTAIN: Did Johansson admit to being the father?

NURSE: He jolly well had to!

CAPTAIN: How appalling! Ah, the doctor.

(*The* DOCTOR *enters*.)

Good evening, Doctor. So, how is the mother-in-law?

DOCTOR: Oh, nothing serious. Just a slight sprain in the left ankle.

CAPTAIN: Indeed? Just a slight sprain. Margaret was telling me it was just a slight cold. There seems to be some difference of diagnostic opinion. Go to bed, Margaret.

(*The* NURSE *goes*. *Pause*.)

Sit down, please, Doctor.

(*The* DOCTOR *sits*.)

DOCTOR: Thank you.

CAPTAIN: If you should cross a zebra with a mare, is it true that you get striped foals?

26

DOCTOR: (*Surprised*) That's perfectly true.

CAPTAIN: Is it true that any further foals may be also striped, even if they are next sired by a stallion?

DOCTOR: Yes, that's also true.

CAPTAIN: So, it follows: under certain conditions, a stallion can father striped foals – and vice versa?

DOCTOR: That seems the case.

CAPTAIN: Put plainly, therefore, a child's likeness to the father means nothing?

DOCTOR: Ah . . .

CAPTAIN: In other words: paternity cannot be proved.

DOCTOR: Well –

CAPTAIN: You're a widower, are you not? And you have had children?

DOCTOR: Ye–es . . .

CAPTAIN: Didn't – being a father – sometimes make you feel ridiculous? What could be more comic than the sight of a father leading his child down the street, or hearing a father talk about '*my* children'? Shouldn't he be saying 'my wife's children'? Didn't it ever occur to you what a false position you were in? Were you never assailed by some small measure of doubt? I won't call it suspicion, because as a gentleman I assume that your wife was above suspicion.

DOCTOR: No. It happens I was not. Anyhow, Captain, wasn't it Goethe who said, 'A man must take his children on trust'?

CAPTAIN: On trust? When a woman's concerned? Isn't that asking for trouble?

DOCTOR: Women are not all alike.

CAPTAIN: The latest researches have proven – there's one kind only. When I was young, I was strong – and, I think I may say – handsome. Two brief incidents keep returning to my mind. And constantly they reaffirm all my apprehensions. I was once travelling aboard a steamer. While I was sitting with some friends in the saloon, in came a young stewardess. She was in tears, and she sat down opposite me and immediately started telling us that her fiancé had been drowned at sea. We

27

all sympathized and I ordered champagne. After the second glass, I touched her foot; after the fourth, her knee. Before morning, I had consoled her completely.

DOCTOR: Every barrel has a rotten apple.

CAPTAIN: Let me tell you about the second. And this apple was really putrid. I was in Lysenkil. A young woman was staying there with her children. Her husband was away in town. She was a woman of the most circumspect principles. Most devout. There was such eagerness in the morality she preached to me, I accepted her faith without question. I lent her a book and then a couple more and when she was leaving, she returned them – a somewhat rare courtesy with most people. Three months later, leafing through one of the books, I discovered a calling card. And on it was written a palpably unambiguous message. Oh, it was innocent enough – as innocent, that is, as an intimation of love can be, from a married woman to a strange man who never made any encouraging advances to her. The moral of that is: don't be too trusting.

DOCTOR: Nor too untrusting.

CAPTAIN: Caution is all. But that is not the end of it. That woman, with her malign innocence, went and *told* her husband that she was in love with me. That is what makes them so dangerous – their innate dishonesty is totally unconscious. Extenuating circumstances, you say. All right, make whatever plea in mitigation you like, but the verdict remains. Guilty.

DOCTOR: Captain, I think you should be careful. It might be helpful to take hold of some of these thoughts before they become unhealthy.

CAPTAIN: Don't give me 'unhealthy'. Remember this: all boilers burst when their gauges top a hundred. But that hundred mark is variable with different boilers. However, you're here to watch and observe me. If I weren't a man, I should have the right to accuse – or, rather, make complaints, as they cunningly put it. I might then give you the complete diagnosis and, what is even more, the course and very history of this disease. But since I am only a man after all, I can only do like

28

the Romans, fold my arms across my chest and hold my
breath until I die. Goodnight.

DOCTOR: Captain, if you are ill, it would be no stain on your
honour as a man to tell me everything. I am bound to
both sides of the evidence.

CAPTAIN: I imagine you've got all you wish to know from the
other side?

DOCTOR: Far from it, Captain. I must tell you that when I
heard that Mrs Alving heaping praise on her dead
husband, I thought, 'What a pity the poor devil's dead
and can't hear it.'

CAPTAIN: And if he had been alive, do you think he'd have
dared speak up for himself? Do you think that a
husband back from the dead could hope to be believed?
Goodnight, Doctor. As you can see, I'm quite calm, so
you can go to bed without worry.

DOCTOR: So, goodnight then, Captain. There's nothing more
that I can do.

CAPTAIN: Are we enemies?

DOCTOR: Far from it. The pity is that we can't be friends.
Goodnight.

(The DOCTOR *goes out. The* CAPTAIN *follows him to his
exit door, then goes to another, opening it slightly.*)

CAPTAIN: You'd better come in. Then we can talk. I heard
you out there listening.

(LAURA *comes in, embarrassed. The* CAPTAIN *sits at the
desk.*)

It's late but we've got to clear up this miserable mess.
Sit down. (*Pause.*) I went to the post office this evening
to collect the mail. It is evident beyond all doubt that
you have been consistently intercepting and withholding
both my incoming and outgoing mail. The consequence
of this delay has been the virtual destruction of all my
accumulated work.

LAURA: I did it out of kindness to you. The neglect of your
duties was due entirely to this other work.

CAPTAIN: It was no act of kindness to me, and why? Because
you knew full well that one day I should gain more
honour from this work than my duties, military or

otherwise. But no, you don't want me to achieve any honour, since that would only proclaim your insignificance. For that reason, *I* have now intercepted letters addressed to *you*.

LAURA: How noble!

CAPTAIN: Ah, so you do have a high opinion of me, as they all say. It appears from these letters that for some time now you have been setting all my old friends against me by implying my insanity. Not only this, but you have succeeded because now there's not anyone, from colonel-in-chief to kitchen maid, who doesn't believe I'm mad. Now, the truth of my condition is this: my reason is unimpaired. As you know, I am able to discharge both my duties as a soldier and my obligations as a father. I am in full command of my emotions, so long as my will-power is unthreatened – although you have so gnawed away at the works . . . that soon I think the whole machinery will collapse, explode and disappear . . . I'll not appeal to your feelings because you have none. That is your strength. No, I appeal to your self-interests.

LAURA: Go on.

CAPTAIN: Your strategy of incitement . . . has plunged me to such a pitch . . . my reason's set to failure . . . my mind must falter. This is the creeping madness you've plotted for me . . . you've engaged to bring me down . . . swiftly and suddenly. So, we come to the question: what is it that's to your certain advantage? Which verdict? Not guilty? Or insane? *If* I go down, I shall be dismissed from the service and where does that leave you? If I die, my life insurance comes to you. But if I should take . . . my own life, you get nothing. Therefore, your advantage balances upon my life. And my life . . . lived out.

LAURA: Is this a trap?

CAPTAIN: Certainly. It's up to you. Step round it. Or walk into it.

LAURA: You say you'll kill yourself. I don't believe it.

CAPTAIN: Are you sure? Do you think a man can live when there's nothing and nobody to live for?

LAURA: So you surrender?

CAPTAIN: No. I offer a peace treaty.

LAURA: On what terms?

CAPTAIN: Leave me my mind. Free me from my doubts and I will give up arms.

LAURA: What doubts?

CAPTAIN: Bertha's parentage.

LAURA: Is that in doubt?

CAPTAIN: It is for me. And you have raised them.

LAURA: I have?

CAPTAIN: You've dripped them like some bane in my ear. The pressure . . . of . . . circumstance . . . has set them bursting into a flood. Release me from my uncertainty. Tell me the truth outright and I already forgive you.

LAURA: I can't confess to a crime I've not committed.

CAPTAIN: What can it matter to you? You'll have already secured my silence. Do you think a man would go and shout his shame from the roof?

LAURA: If I say it's untrue, you will still be in doubt. If I say it's true, then you will be convinced. You want it to be true, don't you?

CAPTAIN: It's strange – but I do. Probably because the former can't be proven. But the latter can.

LAURA: Have you any grounds for these suspicions?

CAPTAIN: Yes – and – no.

LAURA: I'm to be the guilty party so that you can get rid of me and get control over the child. I'm not falling for that.

CAPTAIN: Do you think I would accept another man's child if I were certain that you were guilty?

LAURA: No, I don't believe you would. That's why I know you were lying just now when you offered me forgiveness in advance.

CAPTAIN: Laura, have some little pity for me. Don't destroy me! You refuse to understand. If the child is not mine, then I have no rights over her. Nor do I ask for any. That's what you want, isn't it? But perhaps you're after something else as well. You want the control and power over the child. And – you want me to carry on supporting you.

LAURA: Yes. I want the power. What else is this death
struggle about? The power.

CAPTAIN: For me, without belief in a life to come, my child
was my afterlife. She made me immortal. She was my
ultimate reality. Take that from me and I am nothing.

LAURA: Why didn't we part long ago?

CAPTAIN: Because the child bound us together. But the bond
has become a clamp. How did it happen? I've never paid
attention to it but now, your calumnies . . . and
vilification are all . . . your entire *campaign* is found out.
We'd been married for two years. There were no
children. You know why not. I became ill. Sick unto
death. Once, when my fever was abating, I heard voices
from outside my room. It was you and the lawyer. You
were discussing the property I still possessed in those
days. He explained the position to you – that you
couldn't inherit anything because you were childless.
Then he asked if you were pregnant. I never heard your
reply. When I recovered, the next thing was we had a
child. Who is the father?

LAURA: You.

CAPTAIN: No. I am not. There's a crime buried beneath all
this, and it stinks the place out. And what a hell's own
crime it is! You ladies have been choked with pity for
the poor black slaves. They must be set free! But the
white slaves, the white ones, they must be in chains for
ever. I have indeed been a slave. I have toiled and
suffered for you, for your child, your mother, your
servants. I have sacrificed my career and promotion. I
have been abused and tortured, denied even sleep,
tormented by care for your future. I have aged overnight
in my struggle to ensure you a carefree life and a serene
old age that you could share in happiness with your
child. I have endured all this without complaint because
I believed that I was the father of your child. This was
the lowest form of robbery, the most brutal slavery.
Seventeen years of hard labour I've served. And I was
innocent. How do you make up for that?

LAURA: Now you're really mad!

CAPTAIN: That's what you hope. I've seen how you've struggled to cover up your wickedness. I made sympathetic voices, knew what the game was. How often I've nursed your sick conscience, knowing that I was only soothing your little recidivist heart. I've heard you crying out in your sleep and refused to listen. I remember Bertha's birthday – the night before last. It was about three in the morning, and I was sitting up reading. Suddenly you screamed out as if someone were trying to throttle you. You were screaming, 'Don't touch me! Don't hurt me.' I banged on the wall between us because I didn't want to hear. I'd suspected you for so long but still I fled from the truth. All this I've suffered for *you*. What will you do for me?

LAURA: What can I do? I swear to God and all I hold dearest that *you* are Bertha's father.

CAPTAIN: What good is that? You've already said the mother can, indeed must, commit any crime for the sake of her child. I beg you, for past memory's sake, I beg you for that death blow, some little mercy that puts an end to agony for ever. Don't you see? I am as a child – helpless. I ask you as if you were my mother. Forget that I am a man, a soldier who can command obedience in men and beasts. Have you no compassion for even a sick animal? I surrender all symbols of power. All I ask for in return is your blessed mercy.

(LAURA *approaches him and lays her hand on his forehead.*)

LAURA: What's this? A man – and crying?

CAPTAIN: Yes, I do cry, as a man cries. Has a man no frailty in him? Can a man's mind and body not be overpowered like a woman's? If you humiliate us, are we not shamed? If you sever our hearts, do we not wither? If you poison us, do we not die? Can a man not shed tears or a soldier grieve? Is it unmanly? Why should it be so?

LAURA: Cry then, my child. Your mother will come to you again. Do you remember? It was as your mother I first gained entrance to your secret self. Your great, strong body had no muscle, like a massive baby, born into this world too soon and unwanted.

CAPTAIN: Yes. You saw me as I was. I *was* unwanted. So: I was born without a will. When you and I were coupled, I thought I had become one. That's how you became the master. On the parade ground I was in command but at home I was the subordinate who obeyed your orders. I became your attachment, a mere ornament to your superiority, your retarded child.

LAURA: You describe it very well. I did love you as my own child. But didn't you grasp the nature of my shock when you would change, when a child's dependence turned into the brutal insistence of a lover? The more passionate the embraces became, the more desolate was the aftertaste. My blood stopped with shame. The mother degraded into mistress! Ugh.

CAPTAIN: I saw these things too. But I could see no opening – for a – reconciliation. And when I thought you despised my meagre manhood, I wanted to force you as a woman . . . being taken by a man.

LAURA: Yes, and that was your mistake. The mother was your friend. But the woman was your enemy. Love between the sexes is a battle. And don't imagine for a minute that I ever gave myself up to you. I gave away nothing. I just took – and only what I wanted. But you had one advantage. I was aware of it and I doubted you to be aware of it.

CAPTAIN: You always had the advantage. You could hypnotize me so I saw nothing and heard nothing. You could give me a raw potato and tell me it was a peach. You could bully me into hanging on to your most stupid, girlish utterances as if they were jewels of insight. You could have dragged me into perfidy, even the most paltry criminality. How? Because you were quite without understanding, you cast away my every instinct and followed your own footling perceptions. When I finally did awake and come to my senses, I realized how my behaviour had been blemished and I wanted to remedy it by some sublime action, some achievement, some discovery or an honourable suicide.

34

I would have hurled myself into battle but there were no wars being fought. That's when I lost myself in science. And now, when I should be reaching out for the fruits of my efforts, you cut off my arm. I am utterly dishonoured. My life is cut down. A man without honour is become a corpse.

LAURA: But a woman? She lives on?

CAPTAIN: Yes. She has her children. But we, like all humanity, live out our childish imaginings, borne up by inspired caprice, by soaring fancy . . . supreme exultation. All that would have been all right but we awoke with our feet on the pillow and by a sleepwalker with the selfsame dreams. When women grow old and cease to be women, they grow stubble on their chins. What becomes of men when they grow old and cease to be men? Those who once crowed were no longer cocks. Only capons. And the hens who had answered that crow-call? What happened when we woke, not ahead of sunrise but perched . . . among bright moonlit ruins. Just like the days long past. It had only been a morning nap of bad dreams, and no awakening from it . . .

LAURA: Pity you weren't a poet.

CAPTAIN: Who knows?

LAURA: Well, I'm exhausted. If you've any more flights of fancy, keep them for tomorrow.

CAPTAIN: One more word. About realities. Do you hate me?

LAURA: Yes, sometimes. When the man in you takes over.

CAPTAIN: That's like racial hatred. If we are all after all in descent from apes, it must be from two different species. You and I. We do not resemble the other.

LAURA: What are you trying to say?

CAPTAIN: That one of us must go down in this struggle.

LAURA: Which one?

CAPTAIN: The weaker, of course.

LAURA: And the stronger is in the right?

CAPTAIN: Naturally. He has the power.

LAURA: Then the right is mine.

CAPTAIN: Can you feel the power already then?

LAURA: Yes. And legal power with it. Tomorrow I shall exercise it by having you put under restraint.

CAPTAIN: Restraint.

LAURA: Yes. Then I shall bring up my child alone, without the bother of your endless ravings.

CAPTAIN: And who will provide for her education when I'm gone?

LAURA: Your pension.

(*The* CAPTAIN *walks towards her threateningly.*)

CAPTAIN: And exactly how will you have me put under restraint?

LAURA: (*Taking out a letter*) By the enforcement of this document, signed, witnessed and lodged with the proper authorities.

CAPTAIN: What document?

LAURA: (*Backing away to escape*) This! The document containing your letter to the doctor admitting to your insanity.

(*The* CAPTAIN *watches her.*)

You've done all that's required of you now. You've played *your* part as necessary by law. Father and provider as presently required. But you're no longer needed. It's time you went. You have to go – because although you now recognize that the strength of my mind is as overpowering as my will, you will not be wanting to stay behind and confess: I admit it! I *admit* it! I admit it! I admit it!

(*The* CAPTAIN *goes to the table, grabs the burning lamp and hurls it at* LAURA, *who retreats through the door. Curtain.*)

ACT THREE

The same as before, but with a different lamp. The jib door is barricaded with a chair.

LAURA *is with the* NURSE.

LAURA: Did he give you the keys?

NURSE: Give them to me? No, God forgive me, I took them out of his clothes when Nöjd laid them out to brush.

LAURA: So, it's Nöjd on duty today?

NURSE: Young Nöjd.

LAURA: Give the keys to me.

NURSE: As you say, madam, but it is really stealing. Just listen to him up there. Pacing – up and down.

LAURA: Is the door fastened properly?

NURSE: Oh, quite safe.

(LAURA *opens up the desk and sits.*)

LAURA: You must take a proper hold of yourself, Margaret. It's essential we all stay calm.

(*Knock on the hall door.*)

Who is that?

NURSE: (*Opening door*) It's Nöjd.

LAURA: Tell him to come in.

(NÖJD *enters.*)

NÖJD: There's this note from the Colonel.

LAURA: Give it to me. (*She reads it.*) I see. Nöjd, have you removed all the cartridges from the guns and belts?

NÖJD: Just as you ordered, madam.

LAURA: Then wait outside while I answer the Colonel's letter.

(NÖJD *goes out.* LAURA *begins writing.*)

NURSE: Listen to him, madam. Whatever's he doing up there?

LAURA: Quiet, while I'm trying to write.

NURSE: Dear God, help us! What'll be the end of it?

LAURA: There. Give this to Nöjd. And my mother's to know nothing about any of this. Is that understood?

(*The* NURSE *goes to the door.* LAURA *opens a drawer and removes some papers. The* PASTOR *enters, takes up a chair and sits besides* LAURA.)

37

PASTOR: Good evening, Laura. I've been out all day. I expect they told you. I've only just got back. Things have taken a turn for the worse then?

LAURA: Yes, my dear brother. I've never been through anything like this last twenty-four hours.

PASTOR: At least you seem to have got through it.

LAURA: Yes, thank God. But imagine what could have happened.

PASTOR: Tell me, how did it start? I've heard so many different versions.

LAURA: Oh, it came with the usual rantings about him not being Bertha's father. It ended up with him throwing a lighted lamp at my face.

PASTOR: It's incredible! Complete and utter madness! What happens now?

LAURA: We must try and prevent any more outbreaks. The doctor's sent off to the hospital for a strait-jacket. In the meantime, I've sent a message to the Colonel. At the moment, I'm trying to make sense of the household accounts, which are a complete mess.

PASTOR: What a wretched business. But I've always expected something like this. Mix fire and water and you've got an explosion. What's all that in the drawer?

LAURA: (*Pulling one out*) Just look at all the things he's got hidden down in here!

PASTOR: Good heavens. That's your old doll – and your Christening cap; there's Bertha's rattle; your letters and the locket he gave to you. (*He wipes his eyes.*) He must have loved you very much, Laura. Whatever else. I never kept things like that.

LAURA: I think he did love me once. Time changes so much.

PASTOR: What's this big piece of paper here? A receipt for a burial plot. Rather the grave than the asylum. Laura, tell me: do you feel no blame in any of this?

LAURA: Blame? Me? Am I to blame for a man losing his mind?

PASTOR: Ah, well, it's not for me to say anything. Still – blood *is* thicker than water . . .

LAURA: And what is that supposed to mean?

PASTOR: (*Fixing her*) Listen to me.

LAURA: Well?

PASTOR: Just hear me out. You can't deny that what's happened suits your book very well as far as bringing up your child as you want to.

LAURA: I don't understand you.

PASTOR: I do admire you, Laura.

LAURA: Do you? So.

PASTOR: So, it's up to me to become the free-thinker's protector? I suppose I've always regarded him as the poisonous weed in our garden.

LAURA: (*Slight laugh which she quickly stifles.*) And you dare to be so open to me – his wife?

PASTOR: How strong you are, Laura. Amazingly strong. You're like a fox in a trap. You'd rather bite off your own leg than get yourself caught. You're like a master thief. No accomplice, not even your own conscience. Look at yourself in the mirror. You don't dare to!

LAURA: I never resort to mirrors.

PASTOR: No. You can't bring yourself. Let me see your hand: not even a shot of blood to betray you. No trace of the subtle poison. A little, innocent reminder that the law cannot reach. An unconscious crime. 'Unconscious' – what an inspired notion. Listen to him, rocking away up there. Take care. If that man should get loose, he'll split you in two.

LAURA: If you're carrying on so, don't tell me it's not from your own bad conscience. Go on then – accuse me. If you can.

PASTOR: I can't.

LAURA: There you are then, you can't. So, therefore I'm not guilty. And now, you can take custody of your new ward, and I'll look after mine. Here comes the doctor. (*She rises. Enter* DOCTOR ÖSTERMARK.)
It's good to see you, Doctor. At least you'll do what you can to help me, won't you? Not that there's much to be done, I'm afraid. Listen to him up there. Are you convinced now?

DOCTOR: I'm convinced that he's become violent but the

question is: should this act of violence be treated as a fit of rage or of madness?

PASTOR: However you interpret this actual outburst, you must admit he's in the fix of some very outlandish ideas.

DOCTOR: Some people, Pastor, including myself, might regard your own convictions as possibly outlandish.

PASTOR: My beliefs with regard to higher things –

DOCTOR: Shall we leave aside your beliefs for the moment? Madam. It is up to you to decide: either your husband is liable to imprisonment and pays a fine, or he shall be committed to the asylum. What are your feelings about the Captain's behaviour?

LAURA: I am in no position to answer that.

DOCTOR: You mean to say that you have no firm view of what is in the family's best interest? What is *your* opinion, Pastor?

PASTOR: Either way there will be a scandal. It's a difficult decision.

LAURA: But if he's simply fined for his actions, he might do something violent again.

DOCTOR: And if he goes to prison, he'll soon be out again. So, do we feel that it's in the best interests of all parties concerned that he should be handled as an insane person?

(*No response from the others.*)

Very well. Where is the nurse?

LAURA: Why?

DOCTOR: After I've spoken to him, I shall want her to fasten the patient into the strait-jacket. When I give the order but not before. I have the – article outside.

(*He goes out into the hall and returns with a large parcel.*)

Would you kindly ask the nurse to come in?

PASTOR: Dreadful, dreadful . . .

(*The* NURSE *enters. The* DOCTOR *unfolds the strait-jacket.*)

DOCTOR: Now watch carefully. I want you to slip this waistcoat on the Captain from behind. As soon as I feel it's absolutely necessary in order to prevent any further outbreak, I shall give you the signal. As you can see, it has these extremely long sleeves which are tied behind the back to restrict his movements. And then we have these two straps which you can then buckle fast to the arms of the chair, sofa or whatever's most handy. Now, will you do that?

NURSE: No. Doctor, I can't. I couldn't!

LAURA: Why don't you do it yourself, Doctor?

DOCTOR: Because the patient doesn't trust me. You, madam, you are the one who should do it. But I fear he has no trust in you either.

(LAURA *frowns*.)

Perhaps you, Pastor . . .

PASTOR: I'm afraid not.

(NÖJD *enters*.)

LAURA: Well? Did you deliver the note?

NÖJD: Yes, madam.

DOCTOR: Ah, Nöjd . . . You know the circumstances here. The Captain is deranged. We need your assistance in looking after him.

NÖJD: If there's any help I can give the Captain, he knows he's only got to ask.

DOCTOR: I want you to put this jacket on him . . .

NURSE: No, he's not to touch him. He might hurt him. I'd rather that I did it, gently – nice and gently. Nöjd can wait outside in case I need any help. You might do that, Nöjd.

(*Heavy beating on the door*.)

DOCTOR: There he is! Leave the jacket over that chair and cover it up with your shawl. Everyone get outside. The pastor and I will talk to him. Quickly, out with you. That door won't keep him out much longer!

NURSE: (*Going out*) Jesus guide us.

(LAURA *shuts the desk drawer and goes*. NÖJD *follows off. The doors are hurled open, breaking the lock and scattering the chair. The* CAPTAIN *enters, a load of books under his arm. He distributes them on the table*.)

CAPTAIN: It's all in here. You can find it in every one of these books. I wasn't so mad after all. Listen to this, here it is in the *Odyssey*: book one, page six, line 215 in the Uppsala edition. Telemachus speaking to Athene: 'My mother does claim that he, Odysseus she means, is indeed my father. But myself, I cannot be certain. Since no man can ever know who begot him.' And who does Telemachus suspect? Why, that most virtuous of women, Penelope. There's a fine thing for you. What about that? Then here we go on. This is what the prophet Ezekiel has to say: 'The fool saith: Behold, my father, but who shall know what loins he springs from?' What could be more clear? And what about this one? Merzlyakov's *History of Russian Literature*: 'Alexander Pushkin, Russia's greatest poet, died in agony not so much from the bullet wound in his chest inflicted in a duel – but from the wounding rumours of his wife's infidelity. On his deathbed he swore that she was innocent.' Ass! Donkey! How could he swear to that? So, you see, I can still read my books. Ah, Jonas, here then, are you? And the doctor, naturally. Did I ever tell you what I said to an English lady who complained about the way Irishmen have of throwing lighted lamps in their wives' faces? 'God, these women!' I said. 'Women?' she smirked. 'Yes, of course,' I said. 'When things get to such a pitch that a man – a man who has loved and worshipped a woman – takes a burning lamp and flings it in her face . . . then, then, well, then you know . . .'

PASTOR: What do you know?

CAPTAIN: Nothing. One never knows anything. One only believes. Isn't that so, Jonas? One believes and one is saved. Yes, that's the way of it. But I know that a man's beliefs can destroy him. That's what I do know.

DOCTOR: Captain!

CAPTAIN: Hold your noise! I don't wish to have words with you. You're just a field telephone, repeating all the chatter in the next room! In there! You know what I'm talking about. Come along, Jonas, do you believe that you're the father of your children? I seem to remember you had a tutor in the house – most attractive young lad. Had the whole town at his feet.

PASTOR: Mind what you say, Adolf.

CAPTAIN: Put your hand underneath your wig and see if you can't find two little bumps there. Oh, my teeth and eyes, I think he's gone quite pale-looking. Yes, well, it's only talk of course but, my God, how they do talk, they really do, they will talk so! But we're all figures of fun, we married men, aren't we, Doctor? How are the hurly-burly stakes in your marriage bed? Didn't you have a young subaltern in your house? Hang on a minute. Let me guess . . . His name was – (*Whispers in the* DOCTOR's *ear.*) There you are. He's gone pale as well. Cheer up, old cocky! She's dead and buried. What's done can't be undone. That's what I say. Isn't that what *you'd* say? I used to know him quite well, you know. At the moment, he's – This way, Doctor. No, look at me. Straight in the eye . . . He's a Major of Dragoons. You know what. Damn me if I don't believe you've grown horns as well!

DOCTOR: (*Upset*) Captain, can we please talk about something else?

CAPTAIN: There you go. The minute I mention horns, he want to change the subject.

PASTOR: Adolf, you are losing your mind.

CAPTAIN: Of course I am. I realize that. But if I could get to work on that pair of crowned heads, I'd soon have you both locked away as well. Yes, I am mad. But how did I become mad? Not *your* business. You're not interested and neither is anyone in the world. Would you like me to talk about something else now? (*He takes the photograph album from the table.*) Dear Jesus, that's my child. My daughter. Can she be mine? We cannot ever be sure. Do you know what you have to do to be sure? First, you get married, so as to be acceptable to society. Then separate immediately, become lovers and then you adopt your children. That way you are at least sure they are your adopted children. You see? But what help is that to me now? What help can I expect now that you've obliterated my glimmering of immortality? What use are science and philosophy to me now that I have no life to

43

live? What can I do with my life now that honour's
gone? I grafted my right arm, half my brain and marrow
on to another trunk because I thought they would grow
together, entwine and sprout into a single, more perfect
tree. Then comes someone with a knife and cuts down
below the graft . . . so that now I have become . . . only
half a tree. But the other half continues to grow, with
my arm and half my brain . . . while I wither away and
die . . . Because it was the best part of me that I gave
away. And now I *want* to die. Do what you like with
me. I no longer exist . . .

(The DOCTOR *and the* PASTOR *whisper together and leave.*
BERTHA *comes in. The* CAPTAIN *is collapsed at the table.*)

BERTHA: Papa, are you ill?

CAPTAIN: Me?

BERTHA: Do you know what you did? Do you realize that
you threw a lamp at Mama?

CAPTAIN: I did?

BERTHA: Yes, you did. You could have hurt her.

CAPTAIN: Would it matter?

BERTHA: You're not my father when you talk like that!

CAPTAIN: What's that? Me not your father? How do you
know? Who told you? Who *is* your father, then? Who
is?

BERTHA: Not you, anyway.

CAPTAIN: There you go again – not me! Who then? Who?
You seem to be well informed. Who informed you? That
I should live to have my own child tell me to my face
that I'm not her father. Don't you know that's insulting
to your mother? Don't you understand, that if it's true,
what shame is on *her* head?

BERTHA: I won't have you saying bad things about Mama,
you hear me!

CAPTAIN: That's right. Stick together all of you, all stick
against me! That's always been the way with you.

BERTHA: Papa!

CAPTAIN: Don't you ever call me that again.

BERTHA: Papa – please . . .

(*The* CAPTAIN *pulls her to him.*)

CAPTAIN: Bertha, dear, darling child, you *are* my child. It
can't be otherwise. You *must* be. Anything else was only
a sickly thought carried on the wind like plagues and
fever. Look at me so that I can see my spirit in your
eyes. But I see *her* spirit too. You have two souls. You
love me with one and hate me with the other. But you
must only love me. You must have one soul alone.
Otherwise you shall never find peace and nor shall I.
You must have one thought only, the child of my
thought. And only one will – mine!

BERTHA: I don't want that. I want to be myself.

CAPTAIN: I won't let you. You see, I'm a cannibal and I want
to devour you. Your mother wanted to eat me but I
prevented her. I am Saturn, who ate his own children
because it had been foretold that otherwise they would
eat him. To eat or be eaten. That is the question. Unless
I eat you, you will eat me. Already you've shown me
your teeth. But don't be frightened, my dearest child.
I'll not harm you.

(*He goes to the gun cupboard and selects a revolver.*)

BERTHA: (*Trying to escape*) Help! Mama, help. He's going to
murder me!

(The NURSE *enters.*)

NURSE: Mr Adolf. Whatever is it?

CAPTAIN: (*Examining revolver*) Did you take out the
cartridges?

NURSE: I did tidy them away, but just you sit quietly here
and I'll soon get them out again.

(*She takes the* CAPTAIN'*s arm and sits him in a chair,
where he remains in a daze. Then she brings out the
strait-jacket and stands herself behind him.* BERTHA *slips
out.*)

Now, Mr Adolf, can you remember when you were my
own little boy and I used to tuck you up at night and
we'd kneel and say our prayers together? Do you
remember how I used to get up in the middle of the
night and get you a drink and how I used to light the
candle and tell you little stories when you had bad
dreams and couldn't sleep. Do you remember?

CAPTAIN: Go on talking, Margaret. It soothes my head. Tell me some more.

NURSE: Very well, my dear, but you must pay proper attention. Do you remember that time when you took the big carving knife to make your boats with, and how I came in and saw you . . . and I had to play a little trick on you to get the knife away? We had to do that because you were being such a silly boy, weren't you? You wouldn't believe we knew what was best for you. Do you remember? 'Give me that snake,' I said, 'or it'll bite you.' And there and then, slowly, you let go of it. (*She takes the revolver from his hand.*) And what about the times you wouldn't get dressed when I asked you? I used to have to coax you and say you could have a golden coat and be dressed like a prince. Then I'd take out the little jacket, which was really made of wool; I'd hold it up in front of you and I'd say, 'Come along quickly, in with your arms, through here. Both of them now!' And then I'd say, 'Sit still then, like a good boy, while I do it up the back.' (*She puts the jacket on him.*) And then I'd say, 'Get up now, like a good boy and walk nicely across the room so I can see how well it fits.' (*She leads him to the sofa.*) And after that was done, I'd say, 'Now it's time you went to bed.'

CAPTAIN: What's that? Go to bed when I've just got dressed? God and damnation! What have you done to me? (*He tries to free himself.*) Oh, you devilish . . . cunning . . . woman! Who would have thought you were clever? (*He lies on the sofa.*) Caught, trussed, outwitted. I'm not even allowed to die.

NURSE: Forgive me, Mr Adolf, forgive me, please. I had to stop you from killing the child.

CAPTAIN: Why not let me kill the child? Life is hell and death's the Kingdom of Heaven. Children belong to heaven.

NURSE: How do you know what happens after death?

CAPTAIN: That's the only thing we *do* know. It's life we know nothing about. Oh, if we could only know from the beginning!

NURSE: Mr Adolf. Submit your stubborn heart and call on God's mercy. There's still time. There was still time for the thief on the cross when the Saviour said, 'Today you shall be with me in Paradise.'

CAPTAIN: Are you croaking for my corpse already, you old crow?

(*She takes a hymn book from her pocket.*)

Nöjd! Are you there, Nöjd? Throw this woman out! She's trying to smother me with her hymn book. Chuck her out of the window – up the chimney, anywhere!

(NÖJD *looks at the* NURSE.)

NÖJD: God bless you, Captain, but I'm not able to, I can't honestly. If it were six strong men, I'd take it on. But not a woman.

CAPTAIN: You can't get the better of a woman, eh?

NÖJD: I could do that all right but it's another thing laying hands on them.

CAPTAIN: What's so different about it? Haven't they laid their hands on me?

NÖJD: I know. But I can't, Captain, sir. It's like you asking me to hit the Pastor. It's something inside you – like religion. I just can't.

(LAURA *enters. She gestures* NÖJD *to go.*)

CAPTAIN: Omphale! Omphale! Playing with the club while Hercules spins your wool!

LAURA: Adolf – look at me. Do you believe that I am your enemy?

CAPTAIN: Yes, I do! I believe that you're all my enemies. My mother, who didn't want to bring me into the world because my birth would bring her pain, she was my enemy. She starved the craving creature within her so that it might emerge a cripple. My sister was my enemy when she taught me to be her plaything. The first woman I took in my arms was my enemy. For the love I gave to her she returned me with ten years of illness. My daughter became my enemy when she had to choose between me and you. And you, my wife, were my most bitter enemy, for you would never rest till you had me dead at your feet.

47

LAURA: I don't remember ever having thought or done any of these things you're suggesting. It's possible that at times some shadow of desire entered into me, wanting to be rid of you, as something that stood in my way. If you detect some method in my actions, you could be right but I was not aware of it. I have never plotted my course. It has simply proceeded in the direction you have plotted yourself. Before God, I tell you I feel my own innocence, whether it is mine or not. Your existence has been like a stone in my heart, bearing down on it and crushing it till the heart rallied and struggled to throw off its burden. That's how it is and if I have unwittingly done harm to you, I ask you to forgive me.

CAPTAIN: Oh, that does sound plausible. Very. But how does it help me? And who is to blame? Is it the fault of a spiritual marriage? In the old days, you got married and you got yourself a wife. Now you go into a business partnership with a career woman. Or set up house together with a friend. Then he swindles the partner and defiles the friend. What became of love? Wholesome, sensual love? It dies in the process. And what is the resultant issue of this passion? Bonds made out to bearer. What about joint liability then? Who is the bearer when the crash comes? Who is the bodily father of the spiritual child?

LAURA: As for your suspicions about the child, they are quite unfounded.

CAPTAIN: That is what's so terrible. If there were foundation, there then would be something to grasp on to – some tangible thing. As it is, there are only shadows . . . concealed, hiding in the bushes and poking out their little heads to smirk. It's like raining blows on the air or shamming a duel with blanks. A fatal truth would have sparked me off and roused my whole being to action. But the way it is . . . my thoughts dissolve into the air . . . the brain grinds at emptiness until it catches fire . . . Get me a pillow under my head. And put something over me. I'm cold – so terribly . . . cold . . .

(LAURA *spreads her shawl over him. The* NURSE *goes to fetch a pillow.*)

LAURA: Give me your hand, my dear.

CAPTAIN: My hand! You've strapped it behind me! Omphale! Omphale! But I can feel your soft shawl against my mouth. It's soft and warm as your arm, and it smells of vanilla, like your hair when you were young . . . When you were so young, Laura, and we would walk in the birch woods together, among the cowslips and thrushes. Lovely, so lovely. Just think of it – how pleasing our life was and how it is now. You didn't want it to come to this and nor did I. Yet, it has happened. Who orders our lives so? Um?

LAURA: God alone –

CAPTAIN: The God of dissonance then – or is it Goddess now? Get this coat off me! Get it off!

(*The* NURSE *comes in with the pillow and she removes the shawl.*)

Bring me my tunic – put it over me. Ah, my tough old lionskin that you tried to take from me. You cunning woman – you wanted peace and preached disarmament. Wake up, Hercules, before they have your club off you. You'd trick us out of our armour . . . false, flimsy protective, you told us. It was the smith who once forged the tunic. Now it's the seamstress. Omphale! Omphale! Raw strength is broken down by cunning weakness.

(*He rises, an effort to spit, but falls back on the pillow.*)

What kind of pillow have you given me, Margaret? It's so hard and cold . . . cold. Come and sit beside me – here, on the chair. That's it. So warm . . . lean over me so I can feel your breast. Oh, it's good to sleep on a woman's breast, be it a mother's or a mistress's. But the mother's is best.

LAURA: Adolf, would you like to see your child? Would you?

CAPTAIN: My child? A man has no children. Only women have children. And that's why the future is theirs, and we die childless.

Gentle Jesus, meek and mild,

Look upon a little . . . child –

NURSE: Listen, he's praying to God.

CAPTAIN: No – to *you*. To put me to sleep. I'm tired . . . so tired. Goodnight, Margaret. And blessed be you among women.

(*He gets up but falls with a cry on to the* NURSE. LAURA *goes out and calls to the* DOCTOR, *who reappears with the* PASTOR.)

LAURA: Help, Doctor, if it's not too late. Look, he's stopped breathing.

DOCTOR: (*Feeling the* CAPTAIN'*s pulse*) It's a stroke.

PASTOR: Is he dead?

DOCTOR: No. He may still recover. But what sort of recovery there's no knowing.

PASTOR: First, death. Then the reckoning.

DOCTOR: No reckoning. Not even blame. You believe in a God that rules men's destiny. You'd best refer it to him.

NURSE: Oh, Pastor, he prayed to God. He did, the very last thing.

PASTOR: Is this true?

LAURA: It's true.

DOCTOR: If that's the case, and I can be no more judge of that than I can the cause of his illness – then my skills are worthless. Well, Pastor, let you try yours.

LAURA: Is that all you have to say at this deathbed, Doctor?

DOCTOR: That is all. He who knows more, let him speak up.

(BERTHA *enters, running to her mother.*)

BERTHA: Mama! Oh, Mama!

LAURA: My child! My own child!

PASTOR: So be it. Amen.

(*Curtain.*)

HEDDA GABLER
by
Henrik Ibsen

INTRODUCTION

I have been fascinated for a long time by *Hedda Gabler*. By this, I don't mean merely the character, but the play itself. For, like most great plays, the apparent central character exists only by the favour of the other characters in the play, however small. I have read the play many times and seen several productions in English, including the lamentable Scandinavian one by Ingmar Bergman.

The first production I saw was that of Peter Ashmore, with Peggy Ashcroft as Hedda. I only managed to get into the theatre by convincing my Pakistani lodger that we were, in fact, going into the Hammersmith Palais de Danse to pick up some girls.

Seeing the play then, and having seen it several times since, it seems clear to me, although this may be a glib assumption, that Ibsen did not set out to write one great part for an actress. Again, as in all good plays, all the parts are good and relevant and essential. Take, for instance, the tenacity of Mrs Elvsted. Hedda Gabler cannot begin to cope with it. Hedda is a *victim*. She is not tragic but desperately needs to get the minimal rewards of life.

She is petty, puny, frigid and clearly unable to carry through any relationship.

The last straw is clearly Judge Brack, who uses her, or intends to. She is immediately aware of this situation and compounds it. She is indolently evil and lives off her own fantasies, absorbing from people better than herself.

The idea of being made pregnant – by anyone, even Lövborg – is repellent to her. Her tragedy, if it can be called one, is that of being born *bored* and that is what is fascinating about her in the annals of dramatic literature. The very concept was unique at the time. She is a loser, whereas Mrs Elvsted is an odds-on favourite.

The important point about the adaptation and production of the play is very simple: the complexity of the character of Hedda Gabler is richer only if the other characters in the play are also seen to be made as rich as they are.

They are all, by any standards, a pretty shabby lot. Hedda is a born victim but she does have the gift of energy, while Mrs Elvsted is a very cold cookie indeed.

What would happen after the last scene? These speculations are always intriguing but, of course, fruitless. The situation is not nearly as open as that of the end of *The Doll's House*. But Nora is stronger and less distracted and commonplace and unable to create her own timing.

As I see it, Hedda Gabler has her fun at the expense of others. She has a sharp wit but no authentic sense of humour. She is a bourgeois snob and a walking waste of human personality. What, for instance, about her honeymoon? What did she really *do*? Of course, she was bored. But, tied to her timidity, she also *chose* to be bored and I think that outset of the play is the core of her tragedy, if that is what it is. Like many frigid people, her only true feelings are expressed in jealousy, possessiveness and acquisitive yearnings.

For instance, she is completely unable to initiate situations in her life. It seems quite clear that the Gabler house would be furnished and decorated by Juliana and that the horses would be bought by Tesman himself.

She always has to be the centre of attention, would like to be a great lady and would be bored whatever she did or whatever happened to her. A great, largely misused play.

JOHN OSBORNE
1972

CHARACTERS

TESMAN
HEDDA TESMAN
JULIANA TESMAN
THEA ELVSTED
JUDGE BRACK
EILERT LÖVBORG
BERTHE

This version of *Hedda Gabler* was first performed at the Royal Court Theatre, Sloane Square, London, on 28 June 1972. The cast was as follows:

TESMAN	Ronald Hines
HEDDA TESMAN	Jill Bennett
JULIANA TESMAN	Anne Dyson
THEA ELVSTED	Barbara Ferris
JUDGE BRACK	Denholm Elliott
EILERT LÖVBORG	Brian Cox
BERTHE	Mary Merrall
Directed by	Anthony Page
Designed by	Alan Tagg

ACT ONE

The Tesman drawing room. Large, furnished carefully. At the back is a wide door opening with drawn-back curtains leading to a smaller room in the same style. Right is a double door to the hall. Left, opposite, a glass door again fitted with curtain, revealing through the panes a glass-roofed veranda and autumn trees. At the front of the stage is a dark-tiled stove. Beyond the french windows a piano. Besides the central opening are shelves containing terracotta and majolica ornaments. Against the rear wall in the inner room hangs a portrait of Hedda's father, General Gabler. There are flowers everywhere and morning sun shines through the glass. JULIANA TESMAN *enters from the hall. Wearing a hat and carrying a parasol, she is followed by* BERTHE, *who is carrying a bunch of paper-wrapped flowers.* JULIANA *is about sixty-five, handsome, kindly, simply but well dressed;* BERTHE *an ageing, country servant girl.* JULIANA *stops, listens.*

JULIANA: Do you know, I think they're still not up yet.

BERTHE: There you are. What did I say? But you just think what time that steamer came in last night. And then afterwards. Afterwards, that was just the *beginning*. The things that young lady wanted unpacked and put away and all before she'd even talk of going off to bed.

JULIANA: I'm sure. Well, let's just let them have a good rest. Relax and recover. Some good fresh air for them when they come down.

(She opens the windows wide.)

BERTHE: I don't think there's really a place left to put any of these. Perhaps here. *I* don't know.

(She puts the flowers on the piano.)

JULIANA: You've got a *new* master now. *And* a new mistress. Dear Berthe, it's not easy to see you go.

BERTHE: Oh, Miss Juliana. What can I say? Looking after you and all. It's been so long.

JULIANA: You must adjust, Berthe. Nothing more. No worse than that. You see, George really does need to have you in the house. Just as when he was a little boy. And after all, you *are* used to him.

59

BERTHE: Oh, I know, miss, but I keep thinking about *her*.

JULIANA: My dear Berthe – now: you really mustn't worry too much on my sister's account.

BERTHE: But I do. Of course I do.

JULIANA: I can look after her.

BERTHE: Lying – helpless there. That new girl just won't know. What to do, I mean.

JULIANA: I can teach her. I'll have to do most of it myself anyhow.

BERTHE: Well, yes, but the real thing is, miss, I mean what I'm afraid of is that *I* won't be up to the young lady . . .

JULIANA: Good heavens, there are certain to be odd things, here and there, to start with.

BERTHE: All her requirements . . . everything has to be exactly so-so.

JULIANA: Heavens, she'd be bound to. General Gabler's daughter! Think what she must have been used to when he was still alive. Do you remember that time we saw them riding along the road together? In her long black cloth skirt? And the feather in her hat?

BERTHE: Oh, I remember all right. But it never even struck me then that she and Master George would ever end up together, well, *married*.

JULIANA: No, I must confess it never occurred to me either. But there it is. And do try to remember not to keep calling him Master George. He's *Doctor* Tesman now.

BERTHE: I know. The young lady – madam – told me that last night too. As soon as she got in the door. I can't quite get used to it.

JULIANA: Well, you must because that's what he is now. Since he's been on his travels. It was quite news to *me*. They were still getting off the boat . . .

BERTHE: I should think he could do anything, that one. He's a clever one all right. But I can't say I ever thought of him looking after people's insides and things.

JULIANA: Oh, Berthe, he's not been made *that* kind of doctor at all. Besides, you'll probably find yourself having to call him something much more grand and impressive later on.

BERTHE: No! Like what, miss?

JULIANA: Ah, yes. If everyone knew or guessed. (*Moved*) If only his poor old father could look down and see how his little Georgie's turned out. Berthe, what have you been doing? Why are the covers off all the chairs?

BERTHE: Madam told me. 'Can't stand that sort of thing.' That's what she said.

JULIANA: But they're not going to use this room for everyday, are they?

BERTHE: That's what she said. He didn't say anything. I mean – *Doctor* Tesman.

(GEORGE TESMAN *comes in. About thirty-three, untidy, cheerful, plumpish but young-looking.*)

JULIANA: Well, good morning. Good morning, George.

TESMAN: Auntie! Dear Auntie! All the way here – at this time of the day. Um?

JULIANA: I thought I should just drop in on you.

TESMAN: But what about *your* sleep?

JULIANA: Oh, I can manage.

TESMAN: You got home all right then?

JULIANA: Judge Brack took me all the way to the door.

TESMAN: How kind of him. I was so worried about not giving you a lift ourselves. But, you could see, Hedda had so much baggage with her and she needed it all at once, I'm afraid.

JULIANA: There did seem rather a lot.

BERTHE: Should I go and ask madam if there's anything I can help her with?

TESMAN: No, thank you very much, Berthe. If there's anything, she told me she'd call.

BERTHE: Very well then . . .

TESMAN: Oh, you might take this suitcase.

BERTHE: It can go in the attic.

(*She goes out through the hall door.*)

TESMAN: Honestly, Auntie, can you imagine, that case is stuffed full of my papers? The *things* I've managed to collect – unearthed, dug out all over the place. Extraordinary . . .

61

JULIANA: Yes. I didn't think your honeymoon would be exactly wasted, George.

TESMAN: Not a bit of it. Believe me. Come along, Auntie, let's have your hat off then. And that ribbon first. What's that!

JULIANA: Oh, my goodness, this is really just like old times. When we were all still together.

TESMAN: I say, what a really fine, elegant hat old Auntie's gone and got herself.
(*He twirls it around.*)

JULIANA: It's for Hedda.

TESMAN: For Hedda? What's that?

JULIANA: That's right. We can't have her feeling ashamed of me when we're out walking together in the street.

TESMAN: (*Patting her*) Always one ahead, Auntie. (*He puts the hat on a chair by the table.*) Now: come on then. We're going to have a little sit down on the sofa here and you and I can have a bit of a chat and gossip before Hedda comes down.
(*They sit. She leans her parasol against the sofa. Then takes his hand and looks at him.*)

JULIANA: Oh, George, it's almost unbelievable seeing you again right here in front of me. If your father could have seen you, now, as you are.

TESMAN: What do you think it's like for *me* then? Seeing you – oh, Auntie! You've been everything to me; *you* know.

JULIANA: Yes, I think I do know. You still like your old aunties. Both of them.

TESMAN: Auntie Rina's – no improvement then?

JULIANA: No, my dear. I don't think we can expect any now. The years don't change. She'll just go on lying there. I keep hoping she'll stay with us a bit longer. I don't quite know what I'd do without her, you see, George. Especially now, when I don't have you any more.

TESMAN: No, no. There now . . .
(*He pats her again. She rallies quickly.*)

JULIANA: But when I think of it – you, George, a married man! And going off with Hedda Gabler, of all things!

Beautiful Hedda Gabler. Just think of all those others
who were after her!

TESMAN: (*Happily*) Uhum . . . I should think there are quite
a few round these parts who wouldn't mind being in my
place. What's that?

JULIANA: And you with your great, long honeymoon – five,
what, no, *six* months.

TESMAN: Well, it's been a bit of a working holiday for me as
well, you know. You should have seen the archives, let
alone the books I managed to get through.

JULIANA: I dare say. (*More intimately*) You've nothing *else* to
tell me?

TESMAN: About the trip, you mean?

JULIANA: Well, yes.

TESMAN: Let's think. Not much, really, apart from what I
already wrote to you. I told you all about actually getting
my doctorate and all of that yesterday, didn't I?

JULIANA: Oh, yes. But you don't, I mean, have any other
news?

TESMAN: News?

JULIANA: Oh, George, come along. You *are* talking with
your old auntie.

TESMAN: Well, I suppose I do have some news, yes.

JULIANA: Yes?

TESMAN: It seems there's a pretty good chance of my
becoming a professor.

JULIANA: Oh – a professor. Really?

TESMAN: In fact, it's more or less a certainty. But, Auntie,
you knew about that.

JULIANA: (*Laughing*) Naturally I did. (*Changing mood*) But
what about the trip itself? It must have set you back a
great deal of money, George.

TESMAN: It did that! I couldn't have ever managed without
my research grant.

JULIANA: I can't make out how on earth you managed to
stretch it out for the two of you.

TESMAN: Well, it wasn't easy now you mention it.

JULIANA: And even more so when you're travelling along

with a young lady. Everything must surely become that much more expensive. That's what they tell *me*, anyway.

TESMAN: It certainly did add up on that account. But then Hedda had to have a really proper honeymoon. She likes things done with style or not bother.

JULIANA: Oh, I see that. Trips abroad are obviously all the rage these days. Tell me now: have you managed to take a good look at everything in the house yet?

TESMAN: I certainly have. I was up very first thing.

JULIANA: And – what do you think?

TESMAN: Splendid. Absolutely splendid. Only thing I can't think is what we'll ever do with those two empty rooms between the little one at the back and Hedda's own bedroom.

JULIANA: (*Slight laugh*) My dear Georgie, I think you'll find you've got a use for them before very long.

TESMAN: Yes, you're probably right there, Auntie. The way my book collection keeps piling up. Um?

JULIANA: Exactly, my dear. It was your books I was thinking of all along.

TESMAN: But it's Hedda I'm really happy about. As far as this house is concerned. She always said, before we were engaged, she couldn't bear the thought of dining anywhere else but in Mrs Falk's house. The Prime Minister's place and nothing else.

JULIANA: And it actually coming on to the market just after you'd left.

TESMAN: Everything seemed to be on our side suddenly.

JULIANA: But such a lot of money, Georgie. There'll be such a lot, for all this, you'll have to pay out.

TESMAN: (*Timidly*) I suppose it really will?

JULIANA: Oh, dear heavens, I'm afraid it will.

TESMAN: What do you think? Roughly, I mean? Um?

JULIANA: I wouldn't like to think – till we've seen all the bills come in.

TESMAN: Well, at least we were lucky to have Judge Brack do it for us on such favourable terms. He wrote and told Hedda he'd managed to get it all through jolly reasonably one way and another.

JULIANA: You're not to worry yourself about it, my dear. I stood as guarantor myself on the carpets and curtains.

TESMAN: *You* did? But, Auntie, what kind of security could you offer?

JULIANA: I managed a mortgage on the annuity.

TESMAN: On your annuity?

JULIANA: And your Auntie Rina's. There wasn't much alternative.

TESMAN: But you must be quite mad. That interest money is all the two of you have to live off.

JULIANA: Oh, come, it's nothing like as bad as all that. It's only really a formality. Judge Brack said that himself. If you must know he was the one who was kind enough to arrange the whole thing. And, anyway, he told me – it's no more than a formality.

TESMAN: That might be so, but all the same —

JULIANA: Besides, you've got your own earnings you can rely on now. Good heavens, if we can't be allowed to help out a bit, just at the beginning at least. What could be happier for us?

TESMAN: Oh, Auntie, you never seem to stop sacrificing yourself for me.

(*She gets up and places her hands on his shoulders.*)

JULIANA: Do you think I have any greater joy in this world than easing things a little for you, my dear? You've had neither father nor mother to turn to. But now, now look where you've got to. It's been hard, oh yes, but that's past. It's past for you, Georgie. You're on your way!

TESMAN: Yes, it does seem to have somehow worked itself out.

JULIANA: It has. You remember all those who were up against you and trying to bring you down all the time. Don't tell me! Well, now they know where *they* are. And the worst of the lot, you know who I mean. *He*'d had his come-uppance, like he wanted for *you*. Stupid fool.

TESMAN: Have you heard anything of Eilert? Since I went away?

JULIANA: No. Oh, I think he's supposed to have had some new book published.

TESMAN: A book? Eilert Lövborg? What sort of a book? But when? I mean – lately? Um?

JULIANA: So I hear. Lord knows if there's anything special about that. When *your* new book comes out, now that really will be something, George. What's it going to be all about?

TESMAN: *About?* Oh, it will be about, deal with, domestic handicrafts as an industry in medieval Brabant.

JULIANA: When I think of it: what a mind you've got in there, writing about all these things.

TESMAN: There's a long way to go with it yet. I've got all these, oh, notes, not just notes, volumes of stuff. It's got to be all arranged and put together.

JULIANA: You're a great one for that. Arranging everything, putting it together properly. You're not your father's son for nothing.

TESMAN: I can't wait to get down to it properly. Especially now – when I've got everything, my own house. Oh . . .

JULIANA: And, most important of all, the one person you wanted in the world most of all. Dear Georgie . . .
(TESMAN *hugs her.*)

TESMAN: Oh, yes, Auntie. Yes, my dear Auntie. That's the very best thing of all – Hedda. Wait a minute. I think that, yes, *that*'s her. Now. Yes? It *is*.
(HEDDA *enters. She is wearing a fine-looking, loose-fitting morning dress.*)

JULIANA: (*Going to meet her*) Hedda, my dear! Good morning. A very good morning to you, my dear.

HEDDA: My dear Miss Tesman, good morning to *you*. We've scarcely arrived and here you are already.

JULIANA: (*Rather put down*) Well, did the bride have herself a good night's sleep?

HEDDA: Yes, thank you. Well enough.

TESMAN: Well enough! That's a good one, Hedda. You were out like a light when I got up.

HEDDA: I should have thought that was rather a good thing, wouldn't you? One has to change one's ways gradually, Miss Tesman. Oh, the maid's left the french windows open. You can't see for being blinded by sunshine.

JULIANA: (*Going to the french windows*) Oh, I'll close them.

HEDDA: No, please don't. Tesman, dear, would you draw the curtains? It's quite impossible to take anything in.

TESMAN: Of course, my dear, of course. (*He does so.*) There we are, Hedda. There we are. Now you've got shade and fresh air as well.

HEDDA: It needs a bit of fresh air in here. So many flowers all over everything. My dear Miss Tesman, do sit down.

JULIANA: I won't, thank you. Just as long as I know everything's all right here for the two of you. I'll be getting on home. My poor sister will be lying there wondering what's happened to me.

TESMAN: Don't forget to give her lots of love, Auntie. And tell her I'll be over sometime later during the day.

JULIANA: Yes, I will. Oh, George, what am I doing? (*She fumbles in her dress pocket.*) I nearly went away without giving it to you. Here, this is for you.

TESMAN: What have you got there, Auntie? Um?
(*She pulls out a flat packet wrapped up in newspaper and gives it to him.*)

JULIANA: Take a look and see.

TESMAN: (*Opening it*) Oh, no, you've kept them all this time for me. Hedda, isn't that *good*? It's very touching, Auntie. Um?

HEDDA: (*Turned away*) I'm sorry, Tesman, what was that?

TESMAN: My slippers. My old slippers!

HEDDA: Oh, them. Yes, I remember. You used to talk about them all the time while we were away.

TESMAN: Well, I did miss them. Look!
(*She turns to the stove.*)

HEDDA: I feel I know them already.
(TESMAN *follows her.*)

TESMAN: Honestly, Hedda, old Auntie Rina's sat herself up in bed somehow and actually embroidered them for me. I can't tell you the things they bring back.

HEDDA: For you. But not me.

JULIANA: What Hedda says there is true, George.

TESMAN: I only thought that now she's one of us . . .

HEDDA: (*Interrupting*) Tesman, I cannot see what we're going to do with this maid.

JULIANA: Do? What, with Berthe?

TESMAN: My dearest, what are you thinking of? Um?

HEDDA: Well, there! She's left some old hat of hers lying on that chair.

(*Alarmed, he lets the slippers drop.*)

TESMAN: But, Hedda . . .

HEDDA: Supposing someone should come in here and see *that*!

TESMAN: Hedda, that hat's – Auntie's.

HEDDA: Really?

JULIANA: Yes, Hedda, my dear. And not a very old one either.

HEDDA: I'm afraid I didn't look at it much, Miss Tesman.

JULIANA: Actually, this is the first time I've really gone out in it. And that's the truth of it.

TESMAN: Jolly smart it is. I think so. Splendid.

JULIANA: Oh, I dare say it'll do. (*Looking round*) Where's my parasol? Ah, there we are. *That*'s mine as well. (*To self*) Not Berthe's.

TESMAN: A new parasol as well. What about that, Hedda. Um?

HEDDA: They're both very pretty and quite charming.

TESMAN: Aren't they? Auntie, do just take a good look at Hedda before you go. Isn't she beautiful?

JULIANA: My dear, there's nothing new about that. She's been a true beauty from the day she was born.

(*She nods and goes towards right.* TESMAN *follows.*)

TESMAN: But haven't you noticed, Auntie, there's something extra specially beautiful about her now? Filled out somehow?

HEDDA: (*Crossing*) Oh, do leave it!

JULIANA: Filled out?

HEDDA: Please!

TESMAN: You can't see properly with that dress she's got on. But I've got a pretty good idea.

HEDDA: No, you don't. You don't have any kind of pretty good idea.

TESMAN: Mind you, that mountain air up there in the Tyrol . . .

HEDDA: (*Very curtly*) I am no different now from what I was when I went away.

TESMAN: That's what *you* keep saying. I happen to think differently. What do you say, Auntie?

(JULIANA, *with clasped hands, stares at* HEDDA.)

JULIANA: Beautiful. Quite beautiful is what I say. Beautiful Hedda.

(*She draws* HEDDA's *head down with both hands and kisses the top of her head.*)

May God bless and keep you, Hedda Tesman. For Georgie's sake.

HEDDA: (*Extricating herself with care*) Oh, do let me go.

JULIANA: Now that I've seen you both, I'll come and visit you every day.

TESMAN: Yes, Auntie, do that, won't you. Um?

JULIANA: Goodbye then! Goodbye.

(*She goes out into the hall,* TESMAN *following, still going on about his other auntie and the slippers.* HEDDA *paces the stage, raising her arms at one point, fists clenched. She flings back the french window curtains and looks out. Presently* TESMAN *returns and closes the door behind him. He looks at* HEDDA *and picks up the slippers from the floor.*)

TESMAN: What's that you're looking at then, Hedda?

HEDDA: (*Controlled by now*) Just at the leaves. They look so yellow – and shrivelled.

(TESMAN *wraps the slippers and puts them on the table.*)

TESMAN: Yes. Well, we must be well into September by now.

HEDDA: (*Agitated again*) Yes. Well into September.

TESMAN: I thought Auntie seemed a bit odd, didn't you? Sort of over formal and polite. Can't think what's the matter with her. Can you? Um?

HEDDA: I've no idea. Is she usually like that?

TESMAN: Not like today, no.

HEDDA: (*Moving from the french windows*) Do you think she was upset by the hat business?

69

TESMAN: I can't think so. Just at the very first, maybe.

HEDDA: I think it's a little strange, throwing one's hat about in someone else's drawing room. Do people do that kind of thing?

TESMAN: I'm sure Auntie certainly doesn't usually.

HEDDA: Oh, well, I'll put things right between us again.

TESMAN: Hedda, would you really?

HEDDA: When you go there later, you can ask *her* over here this evening.

TESMAN: I'll do that, and, just one other thing if you could do it.

HEDDA: Yes?

TESMAN: Only – if you could find your way to calling her 'Auntie'. Um? Just for me, Hedda.

HEDDA: No, Tesman, I'm sorry. You simply can't ask me to do that; I've told you. I might manage 'Aunt' sometimes, but that's about as far as it goes.

TESMAN: Of course, that'll be fine then. I just thought what with being one of us now . . .

HEDDA: Oh, I just don't *know*.
    (*She crosses centre. He follows her.*)

TESMAN: There's nothing wrong is there, Hedda? Um?

HEDDA: I'm only taking a look at my old piano. It doesn't fit in here.

TESMAN: As soon as my money starts coming in, you'll get a new one, you see.

HEDDA: No, you mustn't do that. I don't want to part with it. It could go into that room at the back there. Better for it. Then, when the time comes, we can have something better in here.

TESMAN: (*Uneasy*) Well – we could . . .

HEDDA: (*Taking the flowers off the piano*) These weren't here when we got in last night.

TESMAN: I expect Auntie dropped them in with her this morning.

HEDDA: There's a card with them. (*Reads:*) 'Will come back again later in the day.' Have you any idea who it's from?

TESMAN: No. Who is it then? Um?

HEDDA: It's signed. 'Mrs Elvsted.'

TESMAN: Mrs Elvsted? I say. Miss Rysing, she used to be, didn't she?

HEDDA: That's right. The one with the irritating hair she used to toss in everyone's face. One of your old flames, was she not?

TESMAN: (*Laughs*) *That* didn't last. Anyway, Hedda, it was ages before I even knew *you*. But fancy her being here!

HEDDA: And calling on *us* as well. I only just knew her when we were at school.

TESMAN: I haven't seen much of her either. Oh, I don't know when. I don't know what she does with herself, stuck out there in the back of nowhere. Um?

HEDDA: (*Thinks; then, suddenly*) George, tell me, doesn't *he* live up in those parts somewhere? You know: Eilert Lövborg, I mean.

TESMAN: So he does. He lives somewhere up that way.

(BERTHE *enters from the hall.*)

BERTHE: Excuse me, madam. That lady's here again. The one who left the flowers behind. Those you've got in your hand, madam.

HEDDA: Is she? Then go and ask her to come in.

(BERTHE *opens the door for* MRS ELVSTED *and goes out. Fragile, a little intense and questioning, she is slightly younger than* HEDDA *but the careful taste of her dress is also less bold than* HEDDA's.)

(*Welcoming*) My dear Mrs Elvsted! And how are you? How very nice of you to call on us and after such a long time.

MRS ELVSTED: (*Nervous, but in control*) It *is* a *long* time.

TESMAN: (*Offering his hand*) For us both!

HEDDA: Thank you so much for your beautiful flowers.

MRS ELVSTED: Please don't. I meant to bring them yesterday afternoon. But they told me you still hadn't got back.

TESMAN: You only just got here then? Um?

MRS ELVSTED: I got here at lunchtime yesterday. I got quite upset when I heard that you weren't back yet.

HEDDA: Upset? But why?

TESMAN: I *am* sorry, Mrs Rysing – Elvsted, I mean.

HEDDA: There's nothing the matter, I hope, is there?

MRS ELVSTED: Yes, there is. And there's no one here, excepting you, I can turn to.

(HEDDA *puts the flowers on the table*.)

HEDDA: Come along then. Sit down with me here on the sofa.

MRS ELVSTED: I'm too restless. I can't.

HEDDA: Nonsense. Come now.

(*She guides* MRS ELVSTED *down beside her*.)

TESMAN: Well, what's going on then, Mrs . . .

HEDDA: Has something particular happened up there for you?

MRS ELVSTED: Yes. Well, and no. Oh, I do want to be certain you don't misunderstand . . .

HEDDA: Very well, then. But out with it, Mrs Elvsted.

TESMAN: I mean, that *is* the reason for your coming, isn't it?

MRS ELVSTED: Yes. It is, indeed. I'd better tell you now: Eilert Lövborg is here as well.

HEDDA: Lövborg? He's *here*?

TESMAN: He's not! You hear that, Hedda?

HEDDA: I hear very well, thank you!

MRS ELVSTED: He's been here for a whole week. Think of it. In a place like this. All on his own. And surrounded by the dregs, you can be sure.

HEDDA: But, Mrs Elvsted, my dear, what has all this got to do with you?

MRS ELVSTED: (*Frightened; quickly*) He's been the children's tutor. Looked after them, in fact.

HEDDA: Yours?

MRS ELVSTED: They're my husband's children. I don't have any.

HEDDA: Oh – *step*children.

TESMAN: (*Unsure*) I don't quite know how to put it – but was he reliable? That is, could you depend on his, well, way of life and all that, regular and so on, to be put in charge of, care of, children? Um?

MRS ELVSTED: For two years past there's been nothing. Nothing to concern oneself with at all.

TESMAN: Is that so? What do you think of that then, Hedda?

HEDDA: I'm listening.

MRS ELVSTED: There's been nothing, believe me. Not in any way at all. But now he's here, in a big town like this. And with so much money on him. I'm just so afraid for him, that's all.

TESMAN: But why didn't he stay up there with you and your husband?

MRS ELVSTED: Once his book had come out, he didn't seem able to contain himself any longer.

TESMAN: Yes, of course, his book, it came out. Auntie was telling me . . .

MRS ELVSTED: All about the development of culture. Oh, civilization itself, and on *such* a scale! That was a couple of weeks ago and everyone's been buying it or talking about it ever since. It's roused such attention, I can't tell you.

TESMAN: Has it really? What is it: from something he was doing before?

MRS ELVSTED: You mean younger?

TESMAN: Yes.

MRS ELVSTED: No. He did the whole thing, all of it, after he came up to us. A year ago.

TESMAN: But that's wonderful! I say, Hedda, what about *that*!

MRS ELVSTED: If only he can keep on with it.

HEDDA: Have you seen him since you got here?

MRS ELVSTED: Not yet, no. It was so difficult getting hold of his address. Then this morning I finally found him.

HEDDA: (*Looking inquiringly*) It does seem a little strange to me that your husband, well . . .

MRS ELVSTED: What about him?

HEDDA: Only that he should send *you* on an errand like this instead of coming to see his friend for himself.

MRS ELVSTED: Oh, but you see my husband doesn't have the time. Besides which – there was some shopping I simply had to get done.

HEDDA: (*Smiling a little*) Then that's different, isn't it?

MRS ELVSTED: (*Getting up anxiously*) Mr Tesman, I've come to ask you, please to be kindly to Lövborg if he calls on you. And I know he will. Well, you were such good

friends once. And from what little I know about it,
you're both more or less engaged in the same field of
work.

TESMAN: We were at one time, that's true.

MRS ELVSTED: Which is why I am begging you to keep *your*
eye on him now. Could you, would you promise me, Mr
Tesman?

TESMAN: I shall be only too pleased, Mrs Rysing.

HEDDA: Elvsted.

TESMAN: Whatever it's possible for me to do for Eilert, I
shall do. Rely on it.

MRS ELVSTED: Oh, that's wonderfully kind of you. (*She
presses his hands.*) Thank you. I can't thank you enough.
(*Frightened*) My husband's so very fond of him.
(HEDDA *rises.*)

HEDDA: You'd better drop him a line, Tesman. Otherwise,
he may not come to see you of his own accord.

TESMAN: Yes, that's probably the best idea, Hedda? Don't
you think?

HEDDA: Then you'd better get off and do it. Now – rather
than later.

MRS ELVSTED: Oh, please, do you think you could!

TESMAN: Right, straight away then. Have you got his address
with you, Mrs er – ?

MRS ELVSTED: Here.
(*She hands him a piece of paper.*)

TESMAN: Jolly good. Right then, well, I'll go in and . . .
Good, seen my slippers, Hedda? Oh, here we are.
(*He picks up the packet on his way to go.*)

HEDDA: Make it sound warm and friendly. Not too short.

TESMAN: Oh, I will.

MRS ELVSTED: But you won't say anything about my coming
to see you?

TESMAN: I'm not likely to do anything like that, am I? Um?
(*He goes out through the back room to the right.* HEDDA,
smiling, goes up to MRS ELVSTED *and speaks softly.*)

HEDDA: There now. That's two birds we've killed with one
stone.

MRS ELVSTED: How do you mean?

HEDDA: You mean you hadn't noticed I wanted to get him out of the room?

MRS ELVSTED: So that he could get the letter off? Why, yes.

HEDDA: And so that I could talk to you on your own.

MRS ELVSTED: (*Confused*) About this?

HEDDA: Precisely. About all this.

MRS ELVSTED: (*Alarmed*) But there isn't any more, Mrs Tesman. That's all there is.

HEDDA: I think not. In fact, I think there's a great deal more. Come and sit down here with me and we'll have a little chat together.

(*She forces* MRS ELVSTED *down into an armchair by the stove and seats herself on a stool.* MRS ELVSTED *glances at her watch.*)

MRS ELVSTED: Mrs Tesman, it's really time I was going.

HEDDA: There's no rush. So. Tell me, how is everything at home then?

MRS ELVSTED: It's not something I want to discuss.

HEDDA: But surely with me you can, my dear. Good heavens, we did go to school together.

MRS ELVSTED: Yes. But then you were always at least one form ahead of me. You didn't even know how frightened of you I was then.

HEDDA: Frightened? Of me?

MRS ELVSTED: Yes, truly. Frightened. Whenever I used to pass you on the stairs you used to pull my hair.

HEDDA: No, did I really?

MRS ELVSTED: Yes. And you said once you'd like to put a match to it and burn the whole lot off.

HEDDA: That was just a joke.

MRS ELVSTED: Yes. But I was awfully stupid at that stage. And since that time, we've, well, drifted apart completely. Different sorts of life, different friends.

HEDDA: Then we must try drifting back together again. Listen now: when we were both at that school, we called each other by Christian names.

MRS ELVSTED: You're quite wrong there. We never did.

HEDDA: But we did, I'm sure. I remember it all quite clearly. I'd like us to confide in one another again. Just like the

75

old days. (*She moves near on her stool.*) Now then. (*She kisses her on the cheek.*) Friends? Yes? And you must call me Hedda.

(MRS ELVSTED *grasps her hands eagerly.*)

MRS ELVSTED: Oh, you're being so kind. I'm not used to this sort of thing.

HEDDA: There, come along, there! And I shall call you Thora again.

MRS ELVSTED: My name is *Thea*.

HEDDA: Yes. That's right. I meant Thea, of course. (*Sympathetic glance.*) So you're not accustomed to people being friendly, Thea? Not at home then?

MRS ELVSTED: Home! If I had one! But I don't. I never have.

HEDDA: (*Looking at her*) I had an idea things were a bit like this.

MRS ELVSTED: (*Staring helplessly*) Yes . . . yes . . . yes . . .

HEDDA: I can't remember exactly now. But didn't you start off as Mr Elvsted's housekeeper?

MRS ELVSTED: Actually, it was to have been governess. But his wife – his then wife, I mean – was ill and more or less confined to bed the whole time. So I found myself taking on the whole house as well.

HEDDA: So that you became, in fact, the mistress of the house.

MRS ELVSTED: (*Heavily*) That's how it turned out.

HEDDA: Let's see: that was how long ago – roughly?

MRS ELVSTED: Since I got married?

HEDDA: Yes.

MRS ELVSTED: Oh, five years.

HEDDA: Yes, it would be, wouldn't it?

MRS ELVSTED: Oh, those five years. Especially the last two or three. Oh, Mrs Tesman, if you only knew . . .

(HEDDA *slaps her hand gently.*)

HEDDA: *Mrs* Tesman! You've forgotten already! Thea!

MRS ELVSTED: Yes. I'll try. If there was any way you could ever know.

HEDDA: (*Suddenly*) Eilert Lövborg has been up there for about three years, hasn't he?

MRS ELVSTED: (*Uncertainly*) Eilert Lövborg? Why, yes.

HEDDA: Had you known him from before? When you were here?

MRS ELVSTED: Hardly at all. Except by name, that is.

HEDDA: But when you were up there, he'd come and see you?

MRS ELVSTED: We saw him every day. He gave the children their lessons. I found I couldn't cope with that and the house as well.

HEDDA: Yes, I can understand that quite well. And what about your husband? I suppose being on the bench must have taken him away from you quite a lot?

MRS ELVSTED: He was always having to travel from one part of his district to another.

(HEDDA *leans against the armchair.*)

HEDDA: Poor little Thea. Dear, sweet Thea. Well now: you must tell me the whole thing, detail by detail, mind.

MRS ELVSTED: What details?

HEDDA: For instance, just to start with: what sort of man is your husband, Thea? To really be with, that is, day and night. Does he look after you?

MRS ELVSTED: (*Side-stepping*) He does everything he can.

HEDDA: I should have thought he'd be a little on the old side for you. What is he – twenty years older?

MRS ELVSTED: (*Irritated*) There's that, and all kinds of other things as well. In fact, you could say that he and I haven't one single thing in common together in this world.

HEDDA: But doesn't he surely care for you – in some special way of his own?

MRS ELVSTED: I've no idea. I'm *useful* to him, that's for certain. And I don't cost too much.

HEDDA: Aren't you perhaps being silly?

(MRS ELVSTED *shakes her head.*)

MRS ELVSTED: That's the only way it can be with him. He only cares for himself. And maybe the children – when it suits.

HEDDA: But he must feel for Eilert Lövborg, Thea.

(MRS ELVSTED *looks at her*.)

MRS ELVSTED: Eilert Lövborg? Why do you say that?

HEDDA: My dear, it's simply that if he sends you off all the way down here, looking for him – (*smiles almost unnoticeably*) – but isn't that the very thing you said to Tesman?

MRS ELVSTED: (*Nervous gesture*) I did? Yes, of course, I did . . . I might as well come right out with it now.

HEDDA: My dear, Thea, what is it?

MRS ELVSTED: My husband hasn't any idea that I've come here at all.

HEDDA: He doesn't know?

MRS ELVSTED: Certainly not. Besides, he was away on his circuit – as usual. I couldn't take it any longer, Hedda! It was too much for me up there. Cooped up there I'd have been in that lonely, lonely place.

HEDDA: And next?

MRS ELVSTED: Oh, I packed a few things, only essentials, and slipped away.

HEDDA: Just like that?

MRS ELVSTED: Yes. On to a train. And then here.

HEDDA: But my dear Thea – what a brave thing to do!

(MRS ELVSTED *rises and crosses the room*.)

MRS ELVSTED: What else was there?

HEDDA: But what's your husband going to say when you get back?

(MRS ELVSTED *stands by the table*.)

MRS ELVSTED: What? Go back to him?

HEDDA: Why, yes.

MRS ELVSTED: I'm not ever going back there.

(HEDDA *rises and moves nearer to* MRS ELVSTED.)

HEDDA: You're saying then that you've upped and left – him and everything?

MRS ELVSTED: There didn't seem anything else to do.

HEDDA: But you've done it so openly!

MRS ELVSTED: You can't keep things of that sort exactly quiet.

HEDDA: But have you thought what people will say about you?

MRS ELVSTED: They can go and say whatever they damn
well like. (*She sits exhaustedly*.) There was no way round
it for me.

HEDDA: (*After a short silence*) So what are you going to do
now? How will you manage?

MRS ELVSTED: I don't know that yet. All I do know is that
I've got to live wherever Eilert Lövborg lives. Then I
shall really manage.

(HEDDA *takes a chair from the table to sit nearer* MRS
ELVSTED *and takes her hands*.)

HEDDA: Then, tell me how it happened – this friendship.
Between you and Eilert Lövborg?

MRS ELVSTED: Oh, it started bit by bit. Eventually, I'd
acquired a kind of – hold over him.

HEDDA: Hold?

MRS ELVSTED: He gave up lots of his old ways, friends and
so on. Not that I asked him to. I wouldn't have done
that. He probably just saw that I didn't care for that
kind of thing. So he just dropped it all.

(HEDDA *hides a contemptuous smile*.)

HEDDA: So you've put him back squarely on the straight and
narrow. What a clever little Thea you are!

MRS ELVSTED: Well, he seems to think so. And at the same
time, in his own way, he seems to have made a, well,
real kind of person out of me. He's taught me to think
properly about things. And from all sides and not just
one. Like I used to.

HEDDA: So *you* became his pupil too, as well as the children?

MRS ELVSTED: Not pupil exactly. But he'd talk to me about,
oh, such an enormous number of things. And then came
the very best time when he actually let me take a real
share in his work and what he was doing. That made me
happiest of all – becoming some part of it myself.

HEDDA: And he allowed you to do that?

MRS ELVSTED: Yes. Whatever he was writing – we'd do it
together.

HEDDA: You mean: like good chums?

MRS ELVSTED: Like good chums. That's right, Hedda.
That's just what *he* called it. Oh, I ought to feel

completely happy. But I can't. I don't know if it's going to last.

HEDDA: You don't sound very sure of him.

MRS ELVSTED: There's something standing between Eilert Lövborg and me. Another woman's shadow.

HEDDA: Who could it be?

MRS ELVSTED: I don't know. Someone he knows. Back in his past. Someone he's not been able to forget.

HEDDA: Has he said anything to you about her?

MRS ELVSTED: Only once, in passing.

HEDDA: But what was it he said?

MRS ELVSTED: Oh, that when they'd broken up, she'd threatened to shoot him with a pistol.

HEDDA: (*Coldly, controlled*) What rubbish! People don't do that kind of thing.

MRS ELVSTED: No. So I think it was probably that red-headed singer he used to . . .

HEDDA: Yes. It might well be.

MRS ELVSTED: Everyone used to say she went around carrying a loaded pistol on her.

HEDDA: Well, then it must have been her.

MRS ELVSTED: But, Hedda, they tell me now that she's come back here to live! I'm out of my mind!
(HEDDA *glances furtively at the back room.*)

HEDDA: Sh! There's Tesman! (*She gets up and whispers*) Thea, all this is to be just between you and me.
(MRS ELVSTED *jumps.*)

MRS ELVSTED: Oh, yes, please! For God's sake, yes!
(TESMAN *comes in from the rear room with a letter in his hand.*)

TESMAN: There we are then. One letter, all signed and sealed and ready to deliver!

HEDDA: Good. Mrs Elvsted wants to go now. Wait a moment – I'll come with you to the garden gate.

TESMAN: Oh – Hedda, do you think Berthe could see to this for me?
(HEDDA *takes the letter.*)

HEDDA: I'll tell her.
(BERTHE *enters from the hall.*)

BERTHE: Judge Brack is here, to see you, madam. And the doctor.

HEDDA: Then ask him to be so kind to come in. Oh, and another thing, put this in the letterbox.

(BERTHE *takes the letter*.)

BERTHE: Yes, madam.

(*She opens the door for* JUDGE BRACK, *who enters. He is about forty-five, short but athletic and stringy. Rather dandyish*.)

BRACK: May one call so soon?

HEDDA: Of course one may.

TESMAN: Any time. Judge Brack – Mrs Rysing.

(BRACK *bows*.)

BRACK: Delighted.

(HEDDA *looks at him and laughs*.)

HEDDA: How nice it is to see you in the broad light of day, for a change.

BRACK: Not quite the same – no?

HEDDA: Oh – a little younger, I would say.

BRACK: You're very kind to me.

TESMAN: What about Hedda then? Don't you think she's positively flourishing looking? Isn't she all, you know . . .

HEDDA: Oh, do leave off. I don't think you should forget what the judge has been doing for you.

BRACK: All pleasure, I assure you.

HEDDA: You *are* a loyal one. But my little friend here has got to be seen off first. Wait for me, Judge. I'll be straight back.

(*They all make farewells and* MRS ELVSTED *and* HEDDA *go out through the hall door*.)

BRACK: Well, is your wife pleased with the ways things have turned out?

TESMAN: We can never thank you enough. Oh, a few things may have to be shifted around from what she tells me. And we're missing a few things here and there we'll have to get.

BRACK: Really?

TESMAN: But that's nothing to concern you. Hedda said

she'd see what's still needed. Let's sit down, shall we? Um?

BRACK: Well, just for a moment. (*He sits down at the table.*) My dear Tesman, there's something I'd like to talk to you about.

TESMAN: Yes, I see. (*He sits.*) We've had our feast. Now's the reckoning. Um?

BRACK: Oh, the money side doesn't concern me at this stage. Although, I must say, I think you could have splashed about on the house a little less.

TESMAN: But it would never have worked. You know what Hedda is like, my dear chap. You of all people. I couldn't ask her to settle for a petty-bourgeois pottage.

BRACK: That's the nub of it.

TESMAN: Anyway, it can't be so long before my appointment gets confirmed.

BRACK: Those things can take time.

TESMAN: You've not heard any more news? Um?

BRACK: Nothing concrete. Oh, there is one thing I've got to tell you.

TESMAN: Yes?

BRACK: Your old friend, Eilert Lövborg, has come back.

TESMAN: I know.

BRACK: Indeed? And how was that?

TESMAN: She mentioned it. The lady who went off with Hedda.

BRACK: Ah, yes. That lady. I didn't quite get . . .

TESMAN: Mrs Elvsted.

BRACK: Of course, the magistrate's wife. So, he's been living up there too, has he?

TESMAN: And he really seems to have found himself again.

BRACK: So I understand.

TESMAN: And it seems he's also published a new book. What about that?

BRACK: Indeed.

TESMAN: *And* it's stirred things up as well.

BRACK: Oh, it has.

TESMAN: When you think – isn't that good? He's got so much talent. I'd thought: there was an end of it.

BRACK: So did most people.

TESMAN: I just don't see what he's going to do in the meantime. How the devil's he going to manage? Um? (*As he says this*, HEDDA *comes in through the hall door*.)

HEDDA: Tesman never stops worrying about how people manage.

TESMAN: We're just talking about poor old Eilert Lövborg.

HEDDA: Oh, were you? (*She sits in the armchair by the stove and asks casually*) And what about him?

TESMAN: Well, there's no doubt he must have got through that legacy of his ages ago. And he can't turn out a new book every year. Um? I just ask myself: what's going to happen to him?

BRACK: I might be able to fill you in a little there.

TESMAN: Yes?

BRACK: You must remember he does still have some pretty influential relatives.

TESMAN: Oh, them! Fat lot of use they've been!

BRACK: They used to look after him once.

TESMAN: Yes, used to. But not now, they don't.

HEDDA: Who's to say? (*She smiles a little.*) They do say the Elvsteds have worked wonders with him.

BRACK: And then there's this new book come out . . .

TESMAN: Well, I only hope things all come together for him. I've just written to him, as a matter of fact. I asked him to come over here to us tonight, Hedda.

BRACK: But, my dear boy, you promised you'd come to my bachelor party tonight. When I met you off the boat. Remember?

HEDDA: Had you forgotten, Tesman?

TESMAN: Yes. I'm afraid I had, actually.

BRACK: In any case, you're not to worry yourself because there's no question of his possibly coming here tonight.

TESMAN: Why do you say that? Um?
   (BRACK *stands up, placing his hands on the back of his chair.*)

BRACK: (*Rather reluctantly*) My dear Tesman, and you, too – madam – I cannot let you remain in this state of ignorance any longer.

TESMAN: About Eilert?

BRACK: About you and Eilert.

TESMAN: Then, my dear Judge, you'd best out with it.

BRACK: You may as well prepare yourself for your appointment not coming through as soon as you'd hoped.

(TESMAN *jumps up*.)

TESMAN: What's gone wrong? Um?

BRACK: The appointment itself may turn out to be a competitive one.

TESMAN: Competitive? Hedda, did you hear that?

(HEDDA *leans back farther in her chair*.)

HEDDA: Is that so?

TESMAN: Compete with whom? Not with . . .

BRACK: Yes. With Eilert Lövborg.

TESMAN: Oh, but that's not even thinkable. I mean, *is* it? Um?

BRACK: Oh, it's thinkable. And possible.

TESMAN: But, Judge Brack, that would be heartlessly inconsiderate towards me! (*Gesturing wildly*) I say, just you think of it – I'm a married man. Hedda and I got married on my prospects. What we – my *prospects*. We loaded ourselves with debt. Borrowed money from my old auntie. And why? Because I was as good as given the job before I'd started. Um? No?

BRACK: Well, there; I'm pretty certain you'll still get it just the same whatever. But: you *will* have to compete for it.

HEDDA: (*Still in her chair*) Just think of it, Tesman. It'll be like a kind of bout.

TESMAN: But, Hedda, my dear, how can you talk about it like that?

HEDDA: (*As before*) Like what? I can't wait to see the result.

BRACK: Anyway, Mrs Tesman, I thought it might be just as well for you to know the real position. That's before you start buying up all these things you're threatening us with.

HEDDA: Oh, news like this never changes any plan of mine.

BRACK: Is that so? Well, that must be up to you. Goodbye.

(*To* TESMAN) I'll come and get you when I'm having my afternoon walk.

TESMAN: Yes. Of course. I don't quite know where I am for the moment.

HEDDA: (*Lying back, hand outstretched*) Goodbye, Judge. Until later.

BRACK: Thank you. Goodbye.

(TESMAN *follows him to the door.*)

TESMAN: Goodbye, my dear Judge, do forgive me, won't you?

(BRACK *goes out through the hall door.*)

(*Pacing*) Oh, Hedda, it just shows one shouldn't go plunging off into things. Um?

(HEDDA *looks at him and smiles.*)

HEDDA: Is that what you do?

TESMAN: Yes, Hedda, I'm afraid it is. You can't get away from it. Rushing off on a grand adventure, getting married and all on, well, speculation, it seems to turn out.

HEDDA: Yes. You may be right about that.

TESMAN: Still, the fact is we do have our own proper home. Just think of it, my *dear* Hedda. Imagine! How we both of us dreamed about it, all the time, dreaming, and now, well, we've got it. Um?

HEDDA: (*Getting up, tired*) You did say we were to live a full social life. Everything open to us.

TESMAN: I did, and don't you remember how excited *I* was about the whole prospect? To think of you entertaining your own proper circle of friends. Mixing, taking part. Um? Oh, well – just for now we'll have to put up with one another for a little while. Hedda? Oh, have old Auntie over every now and then . . . Oh, my dear, this isn't at all what you'd wanted for yourself . . .

HEDDA: To begin with: there'll be no liveried footmen, naturally.

TESMAN: I'm afraid there's no point in even discussing it.

HEDDA: And the chestnut gelding you talked to me about . . .

TESMAN: A horse!

85

HEDDA: No, I suppose I mustn't think about that now.

TESMAN: I shouldn't think that needs saying.

HEDDA: (*Crossing the room*) Oh, well, I've still one thing left to keep me going.

TESMAN: (*Pleased*) I'm so glad for that, Hedda. What's that, then? Um?

HEDDA: (*In the doorway, looking at him with concealed scorn*) My pistols, Georgie.

TESMAN: Pistols!

HEDDA: (*Her eyes cold*) General Gabler's pistols.
(*She goes out of the back room.*)

TESMAN: (*Calling after her*) Dearest Hedda, my dear, don't, please! Leave those things alone, Hedda. Please. For my sake. Um?
(*Curtain.*)

ACT TWO

The same as Act One, except that the piano has been moved out into the room at the back, and it has been replaced by an elegant little desk with a bookshelf. A small table has been placed to the left of the sofa. Most of the flowers have been removed, except for Mrs Elvsted's. It is afternoon.

    HEDDA, *dressed to receive callers, is alone in the room. She stands by the french windows, loading one of her revolvers. The other lies in an open pistol case on the desk.*

HEDDA: (*Looking out into garden; calling*) Judge Brack – hullo again.

BRACK: (*Off*) Hullo again to *you*, Mrs Tesman.
    (HEDDA *raises pistol and aims.*)

HEDDA: I think I'm going to shoot you, Judge Brack.

BRACK: No, no, no! Stop pointing that thing at me.

HEDDA: That's what happens to people who try sneaking in the back way.
    (*She fires.*)

BRACK: (*Nearer*) Have you gone completely mad!

HEDDA: Oh, I say! Did I get you!

BRACK: (*Just outside*) Just stop your stupid play-acting.

HEDDA: Whatever your honour says. Do come in.
    (BRACK *enters, dressed for a bachelor party and carrying a light overcoat.*)

BRACK: What, in God's name do you think you're still doing – playing about like that? What are you supposed to be aiming at?

HEDDA: Oh, I just stand sometimes. And take the odd shot.

BRACK: (*Carefully taking the pistol from her*) If you wouldn't mind? (*He examines it.*) Oh, yes, I know this one all right. (*He looks round.*) Where's his case? Ah yes. (*He puts it back in the case and closes it.*) I think we've had enough of this particular performance for today.

HEDDA: What *am* I allowed to do then?

BRACK: Has no one been to see you?
    (HEDDA *closes the french windows.*)

HEDDA: No. Not anyone. Everyone I might know is probably in the country.

BRACK: And not your husband, either?

(HEDDA *puts the pistol case in the desk drawer.*)

HEDDA: No. As soon as he'd had his evening meal he was off to his 'auntie's'! He didn't know you'd be here so soon, obviously.

BRACK: Ah, I'd not thought of that. That was stupid of me.

HEDDA: Stupid? How do you mean?

BRACK: I could have come over here earlier.

HEDDA: (*Crossing stage*) Well, there wouldn't have been anyone here to greet you. I've been getting ready in my room ever since lunch.

BRACK: You mean there wouldn't have been any little crack in the door we could have talked through?

HEDDA: You didn't arrange one.

BRACK: Another mistake on my part.

HEDDA: Well, I suppose we'd best sit down and wait. Tesman won't be back for a while yet.

BRACK: I shall just have to be patient then.

(HEDDA *sits in the corner of the sofa,* BRACK *puts his coat over the back of the nearest chair and sits down, keeping his hat in his hand. Short pause. They look at each other.*)

HEDDA: Well?

BRACK: (*In the same tone of voice*) Well?

HEDDA: I was first.

BRACK: All right, then. Let's have a little chat together – Mrs Tesman.

HEDDA: (*Lying farther back in the sofa*) It seems such an age since we talked. You can't exactly count last night – or this morning either.

BRACK: Between the two of us, you mean?

HEDDA: More or less.

BRACK: There hasn't been a day I haven't thought of you being back here again.

HEDDA: And me.

BRACK: Did you? Really? All I could think of was Mrs Tesman actually enjoying her honeymoon. What a word!

HEDDA: Yes. What . . .

BRACK: Your husband was eloquent enough in his letters about it all.

HEDDA: He would be. Snorting around in libraries is his idea of the very best. Copying bits out of other people's books . . .

BRACK: (*With some pleasure*) Well, that's his lot in life. For the most part.

HEDDA: Indeed. And so it is. And what about me? I've been so bored, I can't tell you.

BRACK: (*Sympathetically*) Is that so? Honestly?

HEDDA: Of course. Can't you imagine it? Never meeting a soul for six months who's got an inkling of our sort. Or could begin even to talk about the things that interest us.

BRACK: Yes. I think I'd find that very difficult.

HEDDA: But what's really the worst thing of all –

BRACK: Is?

HEDDA: Being stuck every minute of your life with the same person.

BRACK: Waking and sleeping.

HEDDA: As if there were much difference. Handicrafts in the Middle Ages! At least that should help me to get some sleep.

BRACK: How did it ever come about?

HEDDA: Me and Tesman?

BRACK: Or Tesman and you?

HEDDA: Do you think it so extraordinary?

BRACK: But not inexplicable. *Madame* Hedda.

HEDDA: I seemed to have danced my feet off. The music wasn't improving and didn't even look like lasting. (*She shudders lightly.*) Perhaps I was wrong to think like that. Or even say it!

BRACK: I'm not sure you really had reason to.

HEDDA: Reason. The words you use! I suppose you'd say Tesman was full of that. Reasonable, respectable, circumspect, impeccably behaved. And all that.

BRACK: I should say he was all those things. What one would call quite a substantial man.

HEDDA: Oh yes, *that*: substantial. And not ridiculous – no?

BRACK: Not altogether.

HEDDA: Oh, he's meticulous enough as a – whatever – historian. I dare say he'll make his little mark there if we all wait long enough.

BRACK: (*Questioningly*) But did you always think he'd become a great success – like everybody else?

HEDDA: (*Wearily*) Yes, I did. And then when he begged me to let him do everything in his power to really look after me, I thought well – why not then?

BRACK: No, indeed, if you were looking at it like that –

HEDDA: It was certainly a lot more than any of my other admirers were prepared to offer, my dear Judge.
(BRACK *laughs*.)

BRACK: I can't be expected to answer for all the other ones. But as to myself, I think you do know I've always had a certain respect for the marriage institution. As far as it goes.

HEDDA: (*Jokingly*) Oh, I never had any hopes where you were concerned.

BRACK: All I've ever asked for is a good group of close friends. Friends I can help and advise when they need it, and come and go in their houses as we all please.

HEDDA: You mean as the man of the house pleases?

BRACK: To be honest – preferably as the wife pleases. And, after that, the husband, too, of course. A three-sided arrangement can be very pleasing for all concerned.

HEDDA: I often used to feel the need for a third one when we were away all the time. Those hours alone together in railway carriages –

BRACK: Well, your journey's over now, anyway.
(HEDDA *shakes her head*.)

HEDDA: Oh, there's a long way to go yet. I've just come to a little halt on the way.

BRACK: Then all you do is jump out and stretch your legs a little, Madame Hedda.

HEDDA: I don't jump.

BRACK: Don't you?

HEDDA: No. Because there's always someone –

BRACK: Someone to look at your legs you mean?

HEDDA: Precisely.

BRACK: No, but surely.

HEDDA: (*Warding him off*) I don't care for it. I prefer to sit as I am. In the same compartment. The two of us.

BRACK: But supposing a third person *should* get into the compartment?

HEDDA: That might be different.

BRACK: A friend you could trust. Who understood.

HEDDA: And was jolly and *lively* –

BRACK: Who wasn't only absorbed in one thing.

HEDDA: (*Sighs*) What a relief *that* would be.

(BRACK *hears the front door shut.*)

BRACK: Triangle complete.

HEDDA: And on goes the train.

(TESMAN *comes in. Grey walking suit and soft felt hat. He carries several unbound books in his arms and parcels. He moves to the table by the corner sofa.*)

TESMAN: Phew! It's hot, I can tell you, carting this lot around. Honestly, Hedda, I'm really sweating. Oh, my dear Judge, there you are, got here already! Berthe never told me.

BRACK: (*Rising*) I came – back – through the garden.

HEDDA: What sort of books have you got this time?

TESMAN: (*Flipping through them*) Oh, just some new specialist journals I needed to get.

HEDDA: Specialist journals?

BRACK: For a specialist, Mrs Tesman.

(BRACK *and* HEDDA *exchange nods.*)

HEDDA: Don't tell me you still need *more* of your specialist stuff?

BRACK: My dear Hedda, that's the point, one always has to have more – just to keep up, if nothing else.

HEDDA: Yes. I suppose one would.

TESMAN: (*Rooting among the books*) Now – what about this one then? I got hold of a copy of Eilert Lövborg's new book. (*He holds it out to her.*) Bet you'd like to look at that, Hedda!

HEDDA: Not now, thank you. I – might later.

TESMAN: I had a squiz at it on the way back.

BRACK: And what do you think – being a specialist?

TESMAN: I tell you, it's extraordinary, the *balance* of it. He didn't write like this before. (*He collects up books.*) I can't wait to get down to this little lot. It's even fun cutting the pages. You know? Yes, and I say, I've got to change as well. (*To* BRACK) We don't have to get off straight away, do we? Um?

BRACK: Relax. We're in no hurry yet.

TESMAN: Jolly good. I'll not worry then. (*He takes the books to the doorway, but stops and turns.*) Oh, Hedda: Auntie's not coming over to you this evening. I confirmed.

HEDDA: She's not? Is it because of the hat?

TESMAN: Lord, no! You don't really think Auntie's like that, do you? It's just that Auntie Rina's so bad.

HEDDA: She always is.

TESMAN: Yes, but today's been really awful.

HEDDA: Then it's quite understandable her sister wanting to be with her. I shall just have to manage.

TESMAN: Still, in spite of all that, I can't tell you how excited old Auntie was. Seeing you after the honeymoon and how well you're looking.

HEDDA: Oh, these aunties seem to be everywhere!

TESMAN: What's that?

(HEDDA *goes to the french windows.*)

HEDDA: Nothing.

TESMAN: Yes. Well, all right then . . .

(*He goes out into the rear room.*)

BRACK: What was this hat you were talking about?

HEDDA: Oh, just a little incident this morning with Miss Tesman. She'd put her hat down on the chair there. (*She looks at him and smiles.*) So I pretended I thought it was the maid's.

(BRACK *shakes his head.*)

BRACK: My dear Madame Hedda, what a thing for you to do! To such a poor old thing!

(HEDDA *nervously crosses the stage.*)

HEDDA: These things just seem to wait for me to do them. And there's nothing I can do about it. (*She throws herself down in the armchair by the stove.*) What way is there of beginning to explain it?

BRACK: (*Behind the armchair*) Not being really happy. That's beginning enough.

HEDDA: But then – why *should* I be happy? Is there a reason?

BRACK: For a start: you've got the home you've always set your heart on.

(HEDDA *smiles up at him.*)

HEDDA: And you really believe that?

BRACK: There must be *something* in it.

HEDDA: Yes. Oh, something.

BRACK: So?

HEDDA: Like I used to get Tesman to take me home from parties last summer.

BRACK: Unfortunately, I lived the other way.

HEDDA: Indeed. Your way home lay in quite a different direction.

(BRACK *laughs.*)

BRACK: Oh, come now, Madame Hedda! But what were you saying about Tesman?

HEDDA: We walked by this house one night. And, Tesman, poor old chap, was humming and harring away, not even knowing what to talk to me about. So I tried to help out this great academic mind –

(BRACK *smiles doubtfully.*)

BRACK: Oh, you did, did you?

HEDDA: Oh yes, I really did. So, just to give him a little bit of a lift-up, I just said in a light-hearted way how much I'd love to live here, in this house.

BRACK: Nothing else?

HEDDA: Not then – no.

BRACK: What about later?

HEDDA: Yes. My little light remark had its return.

BRACK: Light remarks often do, I'm afraid.

HEDDA: Thanks. So, it was our feeling for the home of our dear Prime Minister that brought Tesman and me together. On the basis of *that*, we got engaged, married and then on to our honeymoon. Yes, Judge, I suppose I should have said something about 'making one's bed' – and the rest of it.

BRACK: What a business! And you never really cared about the house at all?

HEDDA: God knows I didn't!

BRACK: But what about now then? Looking as it does now?

HEDDA: Ugh! This room, everywhere, it all smells of lavender and old rose petals. But that's Auntie's doing, I suppose.

(BRACK *laughs*.)

BRACK: I fancy that's the Prime Minister's lately departed lady on her way to heaven.

HEDDA: It's a death smell, that's for sure. It reminds me of the flowers one's worn at a ball – the following day. (*She holds her hands behind her neck, leans back in her chair and looks at him.*) Oh, my dear Judge, you cannot imagine the boredom I am going to feel in this place.

BRACK: But there must be something if this life you can find to interest yourself in? Even being Madame Hedda?

HEDDA: To interest myself in?

BRACK: That *would* be best. Wouldn't it?

HEDDA: Well, I don't know what it might be. I did think – but that's not possible either.

BRACK: Who can tell? What is it that's not possible?

HEDDA: I had thought – for instance – that I might get Tesman to go into politics.

(BRACK *laughs*.)

BRACK: Tesman! Oh, I don't think he's quite got it in him to be a politician!

HEDDA: You're probably right. But what if I could get him to try at it?

BRACK: All right. But what's there in it for *you*? He won't be up to it. And what's the point in that?

HEDDA: Because: I'm bored. (*Pause.*) Do you think there'd never be any question of Tesman being Prime Minister?

BRACK: Madame Hedda, I think I can tell you he'd have to be pretty well off for a start.

(HEDDA *rises impatiently*.)

94

HEDDA: That's *it*, isn't it? It's all this waiting and scrimping and watching. It's all so pathetic. It really is.

BRACK: Perhaps the real reason's a bit different.

HEDDA: How different?

BRACK: There's never been a real excitement in your life.

HEDDA: You mean nothing authentic?

BRACK: If you like to call it that. But perhaps now it might.

HEDDA: (*Throwing back her head*) Oh, you mean this desperate race for the professorship? That's up to Tesman. I really can't be thinking about that.

BRACK: Just as you say. But what's going to happen if you should suddenly find yourself caught up with – what most people would insist – the most tying and demanding of responsibilities. (*He smiles.*) What about that, little, sweet, little Madame Hedda?

HEDDA: (*Angrily*) Oh, be quiet! That's not going to happen to *me*!

BRACK: (*Cautiously*) We can always talk about it in a year's time, say. Or earlier.

HEDDA: I've no yearnings in that way, Judge Brack. I don't *look* for those demands.

BRACK: But, as a woman, don't you ever have any feelings for –

HEDDA: (*At the french windows*) Oh, leave it alone, I do ask you! I often think that there's only one thing in this world I have any talent for at all.

BRACK: (*Closer to her*) Which is what – if I may ask?

HEDDA: (*Still looking out*) Boring myself to death. So, there it is. (*She turns back to him and laughs.*) Quite right – here comes the professor.

BRACK: (*Slowly, warningly*) Now then, Madame Hedda, now then . . .

(TESMAN, *dressed for the evening, holding hat and gloves, comes in from the rear room.*)

TESMAN: I say, Hedda, there's no message or anything from Eilert? Um?

HEDDA: No.

TESMAN: No, well, he'll be here soon then.

BRACK: So you think he'll still come?

TESMAN: Oh, I'm quite certain. All that stuff you talked about this morning was most likely rumour.

BRACK: Yes?

TESMAN: Oh, yes. Auntie says she doesn't think for a moment he'd try to get in my way. When I think of it . . .

BRACK: That's all right then.

(TESMAN *puts down his hat and gloves on a chair, right.*)

TESMAN: But we really ought to wait for him as long as we can.

BRACK: There's plenty of time. They won't start arriving at my place before seven or half past.

TESMAN: So: we can keep Hedda company a bit longer. While we keep an eye on the time, um?

(HEDDA *puts Brack's overcoat and hat on the corner sofa.*)

HEDDA: And, if the worst comes to the worst, Mr Lövborg can sit down here and talk to me.

BRACK: (*Trying to take his things himself*) Please, Mrs Tesman. What do you mean? If the worst comes to the worst?

HEDDA: If he doesn't want to go with you and Tesman.

TESMAN: (*Uncertain*) I say, Hedda, it will be all right for him to be here with you? Um? I mean, you know Auntie's not coming?

HEDDA: Yes. But Mrs Elvsted will be. We can all three have a cup of tea together.

TESMAN: Oh, fine then.

(BRACK *smiles.*)

BRACK: And probably the best thing for *him* too.

HEDDA: Really? Why?

BRACK: Why, Mrs Tesman, you've always mocked my little bachelor nights out. That they were only for those with really hard-fast principles.

HEDDA: I'm sure Mr Lövborg's principles are as hard-fast as any by now. You know what converts are like.

(BERTHE *comes in from the hall.*)

BERTHE: There's a gentleman to see you, madam.

HEDDA: Then show him in.

TESMAN: (*Softly*) It's him all right. I'll bet you. What about that!

(EILERT LÖVBORG *enters from the hall. He is tall and thin. The same age as* TESMAN *but burning out. He is dressed in an elegant black suit. His face is pale, with pinkish marks on his cheekbones. He carries dark gloves and a top hat. He stands shyly by the door and bows quickly.* TESMAN *goes to him and shakes his hand.*)

My dear Eilert! What a thing – seeing you after all this time!

LÖVBORG: (*Quietly*) It was nice of you to write. (*He approaches* HEDDA.) May I shake your hand as well, Mrs Tesman?

HEDDA: (*Taking his hand*) You're very welcome, Mr Lövborg. (*With a gesture*) I don't know whether you two gentlemen have – ?

(LÖVBORG *bows slightly.*)

LÖVBORG: Judge Brack, is it not?

BRACK: The same. We did meet – a few years ago.

TESMAN: (*With his hand round* LÖVBORG's *shoulders*) Now, Eilert, you've just got to treat the place like your own. That's the way, isn't it, Hedda? They tell me you're going to settle down in the old place again. Um?

LÖVBORG: I'd like to.

TESMAN: Jolly good decision. Oh, and just a minute, *another* thing. I've actually got hold of your new book. Mind you, not had a moment's chance to read it yet.

LÖVBORG: I shouldn't bother much with that.

TESMAN: What? Why's that?

LÖVBORG: There's little enough in it.

TESMAN: I say, that's a funny remark coming from the author! Um?

BRACK: All the same, it seems to have done very well.

LÖVBORG: Just as I'd hoped. I wrote a book I knew everyone would be sure to agree with.

BRACK: Very sensible.

TESMAN: Yes, but my dear Eilert –

LÖVBORG: Because now I want to build up an entirely new position for myself. Start from scratch.

TESMAN: (*A little disconcerted*) Yes, well I suppose you might at that. Um?

(LÖVBORG *smiles, puts his hat down and takes out a*
package from his coat pocket.)

LÖVBORG: But when this comes out – try to read this,
George Tesman. This is the real thing. This is the one
that contains me.

TESMAN: Is that so? What's it about?

LÖVBORG: It's the heir.

TESMAN: Heir? Heir to what?

LÖVBORG: The old book.

TESMAN: (*Confused*) You mean the *new* book?

LÖVBORG: If you like.

TESMAN: But, my dear Eilert, this one, I mean the one I've
got here today, that covers everything right up to the
very present.

LÖVBORG: It does. And this one covers the future.

TESMAN: The future! Good lord, what on earth can we
possibly know about *that*?

LÖVBORG: Indeed. But there are some things that should be
said. (*He opens the package.*) There, take a look –

TESMAN: This isn't your handwriting?

BRACK: I dictated it. (*He turns the pages.*) It's divided into
two parts. The first is about the culture and powers that
will produce the future. (*He turns further on.*) The
second, well, that's about what the nature of that future
will be.

TESMAN: I say! I don't think I'd ever begin to think of
writing about something like that!

HEDDA: (*By the french windows, drumming on the pane*) Quite
right. You wouldn't.

(LÖVBORG *stuffs the papers back in their folder and puts
the package on the table.*)

LÖVBORG: I brought it with me because I thought I might
read some bits of it out to you during this evening.

TESMAN: That's very nice of you, Eilert. Only the truth
is . . . (*He looks at* BRACK.) This evening's a bit –

LÖVBORG: Another time. No hurry.

BRACK: The thing is, Mr Lövborg, I'm giving a little dinner
over at my place. Really in Tesman's honour.

LÖVBORG: Well – I mustn't keep you –

BRACK: Not so fast. Do, please, give me the pleasure of joining us.

LÖVBORG: (*Abruptly and decidedly*) No, I can't. But thank you.

BRACK: Come, do, I ask you. There's just a few of us. We'll have quite a 'sporty' time of it, as Hedda – Mrs Tesman – calls it.

LÖVBORG: I'm sure. All the same –

BRACK: You can bring your manuscript along with you and read it out to Tesman at my place. There are loads of rooms.

TESMAN: Now, that's an idea. What about it, Eilert?

HEDDA: (*Going between them*) Tesman, dear, it's quite clear that Mr Lövborg doesn't want to go. I'm certain Mr Lövborg would far rather sit here and have some supper with me.

(LÖVBORG *looks at her.*)

LÖVBORG: With you, Mrs Tesman?

HEDDA: And with Mrs Elvsted.

LÖVBORG: Oh – (*lightly*) – I saw her in passing today.

HEDDA: Did you? Well, she's coming over tonight, so I really do think you should stay. If you don't, she'll have no one to see her home.

LÖVBORG: True. In that case – thank you, Mrs Tesman – I'll stay.

HEDDA: I'll speak to the maid.

(*She goes to the hall door and rings.* BERTHE *enters.* HEDDA *talks quietly with her, pointing to the rear room.* BERTHE *nods and goes out.* TESMAN *is speaking during this.*)

TESMAN: Look here, Eilert, this new stuff of yours about the, the future – did you want to lecture about it?

LÖVBORG: Yes.

TESMAN: Only they said something down at the bookshop about you giving a series of lectures here during the autumn.

LÖVBORG: I'd like to, I hope you don't begrudge it to me, Tesman.

TESMAN: Good lord, no! But – ?

LÖVBORG: I can see that it might be a bad time from your point of view.

TESMAN: Oh, you can't change your plans simply for me.

LÖVBORG: Of course, I shall wait till your job's confirmed.

TESMAN: Wait? But I thought – I assumed – you must be in the running yourself.

LÖVBORG: No. I only want to beat you in the popular sense.

TESMAN: Good lord! Old Auntie *was* right then. I knew it all along. Hedda! What about that! Eilert's not standing in our way at all.

HEDDA: (*Brusquely*) Our way? Don't include me.

(*She goes to the rear room, where* BERTHE *is setting carafes and glasses on a table.* HEDDA *nods to her and comes back into the room.* BERTHE *goes out.* TESMAN *speaks during this.*)

TESMAN: What about all this then, Brack? Um?

BRACK: I think victory with honour can be a fine thing.

TESMAN: Of course it can. Still –

HEDDA: (*Cold smile at* TESMAN) You look quite thunderstruck, Tesman.

TESMAN: I think perhaps I am.

BRACK: There did seem something of a cloud over us.

HEDDA: (*Pointing to rear room*) Well, gentlemen, won't you take a glass of cold punch?

(BRACK *looks at his watch.*)

BRACK: Having a chaser before we even start, eh? All right – why not?

TESMAN: Splendid, Hedda. Absolutely splendid. Just the thing for us at the moment.

HEDDA: And you'll have one, won't you, Mr Lövborg?

LÖVBORG: No, thank you. Not for me.

TESMAN: I say, cold punch isn't exactly lethal. Take it from me.

LÖVBORG: Maybe not for everyone.

HEDDA: I'll keep Mr Lövborg company while you have your drink.

TESMAN: Right-ho, Hedda, just as you like.

(TESMAN *and* BRACK *enter the rear room, sit down, drink punch, smoke cigarettes and talk elatedly with each other*

while the following action takes place. EILERT LÖVBORG
remains standing by the stove. HEDDA *goes over to the desk.*)

HEDDA: (*Voice raised somewhat*) I've some photographs here if
   you'd like to look at them. We – Tesman and I – went
   through the Tyrol on our way home.
   (*She brings out an album which she lays on the table by the
   sofa and sits in the upper corner of the sofa.* EILERT *comes
   nearer, stands still and looks at her. Then he takes a chair
   and sits on her left, his back to the rear room.*
   HEDDA *opens the album.*)
   You see these mountains, Mr Lövborg? Those are the
   Ortler Group. Tesman has written it down underneath.
   You see, there. The Ortler Group from Merano.
LÖVBORG: (*Who has not taken his eyes off her, quietly and
   slowly*) Hedda – Gabler!
HEDDA: (*Quick glance*) Sh!
LÖVBORG: (*Again quietly*) Hedda Gabler.
HEDDA: (*Looking at the album*) Yes, that used to be my name.
   When we knew each other first.
LÖVBORG: So, from now on, for the rest of my life, I must
   remember never to say 'Hedda Gabler'.
HEDDA: Yes, I think you should. Start to make an effort.
   Sooner the better.
LÖVBORG: Hedda Gabler married? And to George Tesman!
HEDDA: Yes. That's the way of it.
LÖVBORG: Oh, Hedda, Hedda – how could you throw
   yourself away like that?
HEDDA: (*Sharply*) That's *enough*.
LÖVBORG: What do you mean?
   (TESMAN *comes in towards the sofa.* HEDDA *hears him
   coming and speaks casually.*)
HEDDA: Oh, and this one, Mr Lövborg, was taken from the
   Ampezzo Valley. Just look at those peaks. (*She looks up
   at* TESMAN *warmly.*) What *was* this odd place called,
   George, um?
TESMAN: Let's see. Oh, those are the Dolomites.
HEDDA: That's right, Mr Lövborg. The Dolomites.
TESMAN: Hedda, I was just wondering if we shouldn't bring

a spot of punch and have it in here. Some for you, anyway.

HEDDA: Yes. Thank you. And perhaps a biscuit as well.

TESMAN: Not a cigarette?

HEDDA: No.

TESMAN: Righty-ho.

(*He goes into the rear room and over to the right.* BRACK *sits there, glancing at* HEDDA *and* LÖVBORG *now and then.*)

LÖVBORG: (*Again in a low voice*) Can't I call you Hedda – even when we're alone together?

HEDDA: Think it. If you've a mind to. Only don't say it.

LÖVBORG: Oh, I see. Because of your love for George Tesman.

(HEDDA *glances at him and smiles.*)

HEDDA: Love? Oh, well done!

LÖVBORG: You mean – not love?

HEDDA: Not infidelity either. That's not on either.

LÖVBORG: Hedda – just answer one thing.

HEDDA: Sh!

(TESMAN *enters from rear room with a tray.*)

TESMAN: There we are then! Goodies!

(*He puts the tray on the table.*)

HEDDA: Why are you doing all this yourself?

TESMAN: (*Filling glasses*) I just like to do these little things for you, Hedda.

HEDDA: But you've poured out for both of us. Mr Lövborg doesn't want any.

TESMAN: Never mind. Mrs Elvsted will have it.

HEDDA: Yes, of course. I suppose she will.

TESMAN: You hadn't forgotten she's coming. Um?

HEDDA: We'd got quite lost in our photographs, George. (*She shows him the album.*) Do you remember that little village?

TESMAN: That's the one at the end of the Brenner Pass. Didn't we stay the night there –

HEDDA: That's right. And got embroiled with those relentless tourists.

TESMAN: So we did! Just to think of it – if you could have just been with us! Oh, well . . .

(*He goes back again and sits with* BRACK.)

LÖVBORG: Tell me one thing, Hedda.

HEDDA: Well?

LÖVBORG: Did you not love me at all either? Anywhere?

HEDDA: Anywhere? Oh, I think we were friends. I mean real friends. (*She smiles.*) You certainly gave yourself out to me.

LÖVBORG: That was what you wanted from me.

HEDDA: When I look back on it, there was something very special – and courageous – about all that *closeness*. Something no one could know anything about.

LÖVBORG: There was, Hedda, there really was, wasn't there! Like my coming up to your father's in the afternoon. And the General sitting there by the window, reading his newspapers – with his back to us . . .

HEDDA: While we sat on the sofa in the corner . . .

LÖVBORG: Always reading the same red illustrated magazine.

HEDDA: Instead of a photograph album . . .

LÖVBORG: Yes, Hedda. I told you things about myself then no one ever knew about. All the nights, God, the days and nights, of doing God knows what. Oh, Hedda, what sort of power was it you had?

HEDDA: You think I *had*?

LÖVBORG: How else does it make any sense? And all those, those roundabout – questions you used to ask me.

HEDDA: And which you responded to . . .

LÖVBORG: But the things you'd ask me! Openly, and with such – ease.

HEDDA: You said I was 'roundabout' just now.

LÖVBORG: Not really. They ended – to the point.

HEDDA: You didn't seem to find it so difficult to answer.

LÖVBORG: Yes. It's difficult to grasp – now. But, tell me, Hedda – wasn't there some little love in it for you? When you got me to try to tell you all I could – at the time – weren't you *purging* me in some way? No?

HEDDA: Not really.

LÖVBORG: What was behind it then?

HEDDA: Are you really so uncomprehending? Can't you

understand – a young girl, suddenly alone with
someone –

LÖVBORG: Well?

HEDDA: Well, wanting to take a look at a world which . . .

LÖVBORG: Which what?

HEDDA: Is kept concealed from one.

LÖVBORG: Was that it?

HEDDA: I think so. And things as well.

LÖVBORG: All you wanted was prying. Certainly not love.
But what made you stop then?

HEDDA: Your own fault.

LÖVBORG: You broke it off.

HEDDA: Yes. Because I could see you were set on letting it
become something else. Shame on you, Eilert Lövborg.
How could you embark – on such a blasphemy of
friendship?

LÖVBORG: Why didn't you go ahead? Why didn't you shoot
me down like you said you would.

HEDDA: I dislike – scandal.

LÖVBORG: Yes, Hedda. When it comes to it – you are: a
coward.

HEDDA: Indeed. (*Changing mood*) And a lucky thing for you.
Now you've found what you really want up there with
the Elvsteds.

LÖVBORG: Oh, I know what Thea's been saying to you.

HEDDA: And do you think I can't guess what you've said to
her about us?

LÖVBORG: I haven't said a word. She's too silly to
understand something like that.

HEDDA: Silly?

LÖVBORG: She's just stupid about that sort of thing.

HEDDA: And I'm a coward. (*She bends closer to him, without
looking him in the eye; quietly*) But now, let me tell *you*
something.

LÖVBORG: (*Tensely*) Yes?

HEDDA: I didn't want to – shoot you down.

LÖVBORG: No?

HEDDA: That wasn't the most craven thing I did that
evening.

(LÖVBORG *glances at her and whispers passionately*.)

LÖVBORG: Oh, Hedda! Hedda Gabler! Now I see what was
underneath. It was you and me! There *were* other things
you wanted!

HEDDA: (*Softly, with a sharp glance*) Be careful. *Don't* assume.
(*It is beginning to get dark. The hall door is opened from the
outside by* BERTHE. HEDDA *snaps the album shut*.)
(*Calling out, smiling*) Well, at last! Thea, my dearest,
you're really with us! Come in!
(MRS ELVSTED *enters from the hall. She's dressed for
company*. BERTHE *closes the door behind her*. HEDDA
stretches out her arms to her, from the sofa.)
Dearest Thea, you can't think how I've been waiting for
you.
(MRS ELVSTED *acknowledges the gentlemen in the rear
room, then goes to the table and shakes hands with* HEDDA.
LÖVBORG *has risen and he and* MRS ELVSTED *nod to each
other*.)

MRS ELVSTED: Perhaps I should go and talk a little with your
husband?

HEDDA: Oh, I wouldn't bother. They're quite happy
together. They'll be off in a minute.

MRS ELVSTED: Off?

HEDDA: Yes. They're out – *carousing*.

MRS ELVSTED: (*Hastily to* LÖVBORG) Are you going as well?

LÖVBORG: No.

HEDDA: Mr Lövborg is staying behind with us.
(MRS ELVSTED *takes a chair, clearly to be near*
LÖVBORG.)

MRS ELVSTED: Oh, this is nice – to be here.

HEDDA: No, no, Thea, little one. You come over here and sit
by me. I want to be in the middle.

MRS ELVSTED: Just as you like.
(*She goes round the table to* HEDDA's *right*. LÖVBORG *sits
down again*.)

LÖVBORG: (*To* HEDDA, *after a short pause*.) She's lovely to sit
and look at, isn't she?

HEDDA: (*Stroking* MRS ELVSTED's *hair lightly*) Only to look
at?

LÖVBORG: Oh, I think so. We really *are* friends. We trust one another. We can say anything –

HEDDA: Anything?

LÖVBORG: It seems so.

MRS ELVSTED: (*Almost snuggling up to* HEDDA) Oh, Hedda, I'm so very lucky. He actually says I've inspired him. (HEDDA *looks at her with a smile*.)

HEDDA: Does he, indeed?

LÖVBORG: And then when it simply comes down to doing things, Mrs Tesman.

MRS ELVSTED: I? *Doing* things?

LÖVBORG: Anything. Once you've said so.

HEDDA: Yes. Doing things. If one only can.

LÖVBORG: What?

HEDDA: That would be – to live. (*She changes mood suddenly*.) Thea, my dearest, I'm going to see you get a proper glass of cold punch.

MRS ELVSTED: No – thank you. I don't.

HEDDA: No? And what about you, Mr Lövborg?

LÖVBORG: I don't either. Thank you.

MRS ELVSTED: No. He doesn't.

HEDDA: (*Straight at him*) But if I asked you . . . ?

LÖVBORG: No difference.

(HEDDA *laughs*.)

HEDDA: Don't I have any power at all – poor old me?

LÖVBORG: Not there.

HEDDA: Oh, but seriously, I think you should. For both your sakes.

MRS ELVSTED: Oh, Hedda!

LÖVBORG: Why?

HEDDA: Or perhaps on other people's account.

LÖVBORG: Others? Oh, yes?

HEDDA: People could think you weren't altogether sure of yourselves. At bottom, I mean.

MRS ELVSTED: (*Quietly*) No, Hedda. No.

LÖVBORG: They can think what they like – for the moment, anyway.

MRS ELVSTED: (*Happily*) Yes, that's true, isn't it?

HEDDA: I thought it was very clear what Judge Brack was thinking just now.

LÖVBORG: Oh? What was very clear?

HEDDA: He smiled in such a contemptuous way when you didn't dare go in and drink with them.

LÖVBORG: Dare! I just naturally preferred to stay and talk to you.

MRS ELVSTED: That was natural enough, Hedda.

HEDDA: The judge wasn't aware of it. He even gave Tesman the nod when he saw you wouldn't dare go to their tiresome little party either.

LÖVBORG: You're saying, are you, that I didn't dare?

HEDDA: I'm not. But that's clearly how Judge Brack sees it.

LÖVBORG: Then let him.

HEDDA: So you're *not* going then?

LÖVBORG: I shall stay here with you and Thea.

MRS ELVSTED: Yes, Hedda, and why not?

(HEDDA *smiles in agreement.*)

HEDDA: Iron clad! Unshakeable – in whatever sad situation. That's what a man should be like! (*She turns to* MRS ELVSTED *and pats her.*) Didn't I say that to you when you came here this morning in such a state?

LÖVBORG: What state?

MRS ELVSTED: (*Frightened*) Hedda! Hedda – now –

HEDDA: See for yourself. You really didn't need to come here because of any . . . (*She breaks off.*) There, now! We can all three of us have a good time together.

LÖVBORG: (*Coolly*) What is it that you're trying to say, Mrs Tesman?

MRS ELVSTED: Oh, my God, God, Hedda! What are you saying! What are you doing!

HEDDA: Do be calm. That awful judge is watching you all the time.

LÖVBORG: In a state, were you? All because of me?

MRS ELVSTED: (*Softly, stammering*) Oh, Hedda! You've brought me such unhappiness.

LÖVBORG: So that was how much belief you had in me.

MRS ELVSTED: Oh, my dearest friend – Eilert! Do listen to me . . .

(LÖVBORG *takes one of the glasses of punch and raises it.*)

LÖVBORG: (*Quietly, hoarsely*) To *you*, Thea! (*He empties the glass and takes up another one.*)

MRS ELVSTED: Oh, Hedda, how could you want this?

HEDDA: Want? I? Are you mad?

LÖVBORG: And here's to you, Mrs Tesman. Thanks for letting me know the truth. Here's to that!
(*He drinks and goes to take another.* HEDDA *lays a hand on his arm.*)

HEDDA: There now, there's enough for the moment. Remember, there's the party yet.

MRS ELVSTED: No, no, no!

HEDDA: Sh! They're in there watching you.

LÖVBORG: (*Putting his glass down*) Thea, be honest with me.

MRS ELVSTED: Yes!

LÖVBORG: Did your husband know you'd come after me?

MRS ELVSTED: Hedda, you hear what he's asking!

LÖVBORG: Was it, was it agreed between you that you should come in here and watch over me? Was it his idea – giving out the law? Did he still want to use me in his office? Or was it my card-playing he missed?

MRS ELVSTED: Oh, Lövborg, oh, Eilert . . . !
(LÖVBORG *takes hold of the glass*)

LÖVBORG: Well, here's to him as well then . . .

HEDDA: I think that's enough for now. Don't forget you're going to read to Tesman.
(LÖVBORG *now calmer, puts the glass down.*)

LÖVBORG: That was stupid of me Thea, all that, taking it like that, I mean. My dear, dear friend, don't be angry with me. You'll see – you'll all see – I went down once but I'm up again. And all thanks to you, Thea.

MRS ELVSTED: (*Radiant*) Oh, thank God!
(BRACK *has been looking at his watch. He and* TESMAN *get up together and enter the drawing room.*)

BRACK: Well, Mrs Tesman, time for us to be off.

HEDDA: I suppose it is.

LÖVBORG: (*Rising*) And for me, Judge Brack.

MRS ELVSTED: (*Quietly*) Eilert! Don't.

LÖVBORG: (*Pinching her arm*) They'll hear you.

MRS ELVSTED: (*Wincing*) Oh!

LÖVBORG: (*To* BRACK) It was very good of you to ask me.

BRACK: And are you coming?

LÖVBORG: Yes, I'd like to.

BRACK: Good then.

LÖVBORG: (*Putting the paper package in his pocket*) Because there are a few things I'd like you to see before it goes off to the printer.

TESMAN: Are there? That will be fun. Hedda, dear, I say, I've just thought: how'll you get Mrs Elvsted home? Um?

HEDDA: Oh, there'll be no problem.

LÖVBORG: (*Looking at the ladies*) Mrs Elvsted? But *I* shall come back and collect her. (*Closer to her*) About ten o'clock, Mrs Tesman. Will that do?

HEDDA: Of course. Very well.

TESMAN: So, there we are then. But I shouldn't expect *me* quite as early as that, Hedda.

HEDDA: No, my dear, stay as long, as long as you wish.

MRS ELVSTED: (*Hiding her anxiety*) So, Mr Lövborg, I'll wait here till you get back.

LÖVBORG: (*Hat in hand*) Very well, Mrs Elvsted.

BRACK: Well, gentlemen, ready for the off. We should have quite a 'sporty' time of it, as a certain beautiful lady likes to put it.

HEDDA: Perhaps I shall come as a fly on the wall.

BRACK: Why a fly on the wall?

HEDDA: So as to hear what's really said when you're all together.

(BRACK *laughs*.)

BRACK: I don't think the beautiful lady should do that to herself.

TESMAN: (*Also laughing*) I say, that's a good one, Hedda! What larks!

BRACK: Well, good night, ladies. Good night.

LÖVBORG: (*Bowing*) Around ten o'clock then.

(BRACK, LÖVBORG and TESMAN *go out through the hall door*. BERTHE *comes in from the rear room with a lighted*

*lamp, which she sets down on the dining-room table, and
goes out in the same way.*)

MRS ELVSTED: (*Who has got up and is wandering uneasily
round the stage*) Oh, Hedda, Hedda! What's going to
come of this?

HEDDA: He will be back at ten o'clock. That's all. All wine
and roses. Full of fire and promise.

MRS ELVSTED: I only hope so.

HEDDA: He will – you see. He'll have regained himself. And
then he'll be a free man for the rest of his time.

MRS ELVSTED: He must!

HEDDA: Oh, I know it. (*She gets up and moves closer to her.*)
You may have your doubts. But I am the one who
believes in him. Now we shall see what really . . .

MRS ELVSTED: You're going for something, Hedda.

HEDDA: Yes, I am. For once in my life, I want the power to
shape someone's fate.

MRS ELVSTED: Haven't you had that already?

HEDDA: No, I haven't. And I never have.

MRS ELVSTED: What about your husband?

HEDDA: Tesman. Oh, if only you could know how poor, how
impoverished I am. And you've been the one picked out
to get the riches! (*She grasps her passionately.*) I think I
will burn off your hair.

MRS ELVSTED: Let me go! Let me go! You make me afraid,
Hedda.

BERTHE: (*In doorway*) Tea's laid in the dining room, madam.

HEDDA: Good. We're coming.

MRS ELVSTED: No, no, no! I'd rather go home alone. Now.
Straight away.

HEDDA: What a way to talk! First, you're going to have tea,
little mad thing, you. And then – at ten o'clock – Eilert
Lövborg is coming back. With wine. And roses.

(*Almost forcibly, she drags* MRS ELVSTED *through the door
opening. Curtain.*)

ACT THREE

Again, the Tesman drawing room. All the curtains are drawn. The lamp on the table is turned down. The fire in the stove is almost out, its doors open. MRS ELVSTED, *wrapped in a large shawl and her feet propped on a footstool, is sunk back in the armchair.* HEDDA *lies, fully dressed on the sofa, fast asleep with a quilt over her. After a pause,* MRS ELVSTED *suddenly sits up in her chair and listens tensely. Then she sits back again, moaning in weariness.*)

MRS ELVSTED: Not back! Oh God – still not back!
    (BERTHE *enters tentatively through the hall door, a letter in her hand.* MRS ELVSTED *turns and whispers.*)
    Well? Has anyone been?
BERTHE: (*Softly*) Yes. A maid's just come with this letter.
MRS ELVSTED: (*Holding out her hand at once*) A letter! Give it here!
BERTHE: It's for the doctor, madam.
MRS ELVSTED: Oh. Yes.
BERTHE: Miss Tesman's maid came with it just now. I'll put it here on the table.
MRS ELVSTED: Yes, do that.
    (BERTHE *puts the letter down.*)
BERTHE: I think it's best if I put this lamp right out. It's smoking. It can go on the table, out of the way.
MRS ELVSTED: Yes, put it out. It'll soon be light.
BERTHE: (*Putting it out*) It *is* light already, madam.
MRS ELVSTED: Yes. Quite light. And no one come home.
BERTHE: Dear lord, I told myself this'd happen!
MRS ELVSTED: You did?
BERTHE: Oh, when I'd heard a certain you-know-who had come back and then gone straight off with *them*. Oh, I know all about *him*.
MRS ELVSTED: Don't shout so. You'll waken your mistress.
    (BERTHE *looks at the sofa and sighs.*)
BERTHE: Quite right. Best to let her get a little sleep, poor dear. Shall I put a bit more on the stove?
MRS ELVSTED: No, thank you. Not for me.
BERTHE: Very well.

(*She leaves quietly through the hall door.* HEDDA *wakes as the door shuts and looks up.*)

HEDDA: What! What's that?

MRS ELVSTED: Just the maid.

HEDDA: (*Looking around*) Oh, we're here. Yes, I remember now. (*She straightens herself up, stretches and rubs her eyes.*) What's the time?

MRS ELVSTED: It's just after seven.

HEDDA: What time did Tesman get in?

MRS ELVSTED: He hasn't.

HEDDA: Not back yet?

MRS ELVSTED: (*Getting up*) No one at all.

HEDDA: So here we are, sitting up till four o'clock, waiting . . .

MRS ELVSTED: Oh, I really did wait for him!
(HEDDA *yawns with her hand over her mouth.*)

HEDDA: Yes. Well, we needn't have bothered ourselves.

MRS ELVSTED: Did you get any sleep?

HEDDA: Oh, yes. Quite a bit. Didn't you?

MRS ELVSTED: I couldn't, Hedda. It just wasn't possible.
(HEDDA *gets up and goes towards her.*)

HEDDA: There now, there. I shouldn't think there's anything to worry about. I know just what happened.

MRS ELVSTED: What then? Tell me.

HEDDA: Oh, things obviously dragged on . . .

MRS ELVSTED: They've certainly done that. All the same . . .

HEDDA: And I know Tesman – he didn't want to come stumbling in in the middle of the night, ringing the bell and making a furore. (*She laughs.*) Didn't want us to see the state he was in, either.

MRS ELVSTED: But where could he have got to?

HEDDA: Oh, I expect he's gone to sleep it off at the aunties'. They've always got his old room ready.

MRS ELVSTED: No, he's not there. A letter's come from Miss Tesman just now. It's there.

HEDDA: Oh, yes? (*She examines the envelope.*) Yes, that's Auntie's handwriting sure enough. So: he's still at Judge Brack's. And Eilert Lövborg is sitting – reading. With wine and roses.

MRS ELVSTED: Hedda – you're just *saying* that.

HEDDA: Thea, you really are quite stupid.

MRS ELVSTED: No doubt I am.

HEDDA: You look deathly.

MRS ELVSTED: I feel it.

HEDDA: Why don't you do what I tell you? Go to my room and lie down.

MRS ELVSTED: No. No, I couldn't go to sleep.

HEDDA: Yes, you can.

MRS ELVSTED: But your husband'll be back soon. And I'll want to know.

TESMAN: I'll tell you as soon as he gets in.

MRS ELVSTED: Hedda, you do promise me?

HEDDA: Trust me. Go in and get some sleep.

MRS ELVSTED: Thank you. Well, I'll try.

(*She goes in through the rear room.* HEDDA *goes up to the french windows and draws the curtains. Full daylight enters the room. Then she picks up a little hand mirror from the desk, looks into it and arranges her hair. She goes over to the hall door and preses the bell.* BERTHE *comes to the door a moment later.*)

BERTHE: Yes, madam?

HEDDA: You can stoke up the fire. I'm freezing.

BERTHE: Lord bless us, I'll soon have it warm in here. (*She rakes the embers and puts on a log, then stops to listen.*) It's the street door ringing, madam.

HEDDA: Then go and open it.

BERTHE: That'll soon burn up.

HEDDA: I'll see to it.

(BERTHE *goes out through the hall door.* HEDDA *kneels down on the footstool and puts more logs on the fire.* TESMAN *comes in from the hall after a short pause. He looks tired and rather serious. He comes in on tiptoes, moving towards the door-opening, trying to slink in between the curtains.*)

(*By the stove, without looking up*) Good morning.

(TESMAN *turns round.*)

TESMAN: Hedda! (*He goes closer.*) Up already! Well!

HEDDA: Yes, I got up early for once today.

TESMAN: I was so sure you'd still be sleeping away. What about that?

HEDDA: Try to lower your voice. Mrs Elvsted's sleeping in my room.

TESMAN: Mrs Elvsted? Did she stay the night here?

HEDDA: Yes. No one came for her.

TESMAN: Oh, I dare say not.

(HEDDA *closes the stove door and stands up*.)

HEDDA: Well? Did you have a good time?

TESMAN: You weren't worried about me? Um?

HEDDA: Not a bit. I just said: did you have a good time?

TESMAN: I'll say. It does make a change. But the best bit was the beginning. Eilert read out his book to me. We got there, oh, an hour earlier than we should have done. And Brack got tied up with various things. So, well, Eilert just sat down and read to me on my own.

(HEDDA *sits on the right-hand side of the table*.)

HEDDA: Did he? Well, tell me about it . . .

(TESMAN *sits on the footstool by the stove*.)

TESMAN: I wish I could – but I can begin to tell you what a book that's going to be. It's one of the most extraordinary things anyone's ever done. It just *is*!

HEDDA: Oh, I'm not asking you that . . .

TESMAN: I've got to tell you, Hedda. By the time he'd finished, something awful came over me.

HEDDA: What? Awful?

TESMAN: I sat there and I knew I was jealous of Eilert. Of Eilert Lövborg. Because he'd been able to do something like that. There it is, Hedda. There it is.

HEDDA: Yes. There it is.

TESMAN: And yet, with all that supreme gift, what hope, what expectation, can one hold out?

HEDDA: You mean he has more pride – more life – than the others?

TESMAN: No, nothing like that. He just, well, simply doesn't know how, when, to hold back.

HEDDA: What happened finally?

TESMAN: Well, thinking about it now, Hedda, I suppose you might call it almost an orgy . . .

HEDDA: Wine and roses?

TESMAN: Wine and roses? Don't know about them. Wouldn't know about that. What he did so was – was ramble out a great, long confused sort of tribute to the, the woman who's inspired him. To write the book. He put it rather like that, himself, I mean.

HEDDA: Did he say who it was?

TESMAN: No. But I can only think it was Mrs Elvsted. So, look to it!

HEDDA: And where did you leave him?

TESMAN: Oh, the road in. The last of us all seemed to split up about the same time. Brack came along as well for a bit of fresh air. And, then, well, we all thought we ought to see Eilert off home. He really was a bit over the top!

HEDDA: Was he?

TESMAN: But this is what I call the strange bit, Hedda. Or the sad part, I should say. Oh, I feel ashamed! I suppose you'd say, just for Eilert's sake, apart from the rest of us or anything . . .

HEDDA: About what?

TESMAN: About, well, while we were on our way back into town, I fell back a bit, you know – oh, not much. You know?

HEDDA: I know. And?

TESMAN: I got a move on to catch up and then, then what do you suppose I found by the side of the road? Um?

HEDDA: How could I know!

TESMAN: Now you're not to tell anyone, not a soul, Hedda. Um? Give me a promise. For old Eilert. (*He takes up a package in paper wrapping from his coat pocket.*) What about that! I picked up – *this.*

HEDDA: Isn't that what he brought with him yesterday?

TESMAN: Yes. That's it! The whole irreplaceable, unique, irreplaceable – thing. He just went out – and lost it. Think of it, Hedda. It's so – so awful. No, more.

HEDDA: But why didn't you give it back to him straight away?

TESMAN: I couldn't – not in the state he was in.

HEDDA: Didn't you tell any of the others about it, either?

TESMAN: Oh, steady on. I couldn't let on to them – for Eilert's sake.

HEDDA: You mean no one knows you've got his manuscript?

TESMAN: And no one's going to know, either.

HEDDA: Didn't it come up later on?

TESMAN: Wasn't a chance to bring it up. We got back into town and then he and a couple of the others sloped off. Just sloped off!

HEDDA: Yes? They probably all went home together.

TESMAN: I dare say. Brack went off as well.

HEDDA: And what have the rest of you been doing all this time?

TESMAN: We went off with some of the other chaps – bit of a scream a couple of 'em – we went to someone's place for morning coffee. Morning after the night before coffee you might say. Um? Well, I think I'll get a bit of quick shut-eye and let poor Eilert recover. Then I can pop over to him with this.

(HEDDA *stretches out her hand for the package.*)

HEDDA: No, don't do that! I mean not straight away. Let me read it first.

TESMAN: My little sweet Hedda, my dear, I really don't think I dare do that.

HEDDA: *Daren't* you?

TESMAN: No – just think what he'll feel like when he wakes up and no manuscript. It's his only copy. There isn't another. He told me that himself.

HEDDA: (*Coolly inquiring*) Can't that sort of thing be written out again? Once it's been done?

TESMAN: Oh, I don't see how you could possibly do that. It depends entirely on the inspiration, the moment, you see . . .

HEDDA: Yes, yes – I see that, of course. Oh yes, I forgot, there's a letter for you.

TESMAN: For me? Really?

HEDDA: Yes, really. It came just now.

TESMAN: It's from Auntie. Oh, Hedda, what do you suppose it can be? (*He puts the package down, skims through the letter then jumps up.*) Hedda – Auntie Rina's dying.

HEDDA: Well, it's hardly a surprise.

TESMAN: She says if I want to see her again, I'll have to really hurry. I'll run over there now.

(HEDDA *suppresses a smile*.)

HEDDA: Will you run?

TESMAN: Hedda, my dear, you could, well, bring yourself to come along with me? Um?

(HEDDA *gets up, tired and repelled*.)

HEDDA: No. Please don't ask me to do that sort of thing. I don't want to be watching illness and death. I can't bear things that are ugly.

TESMAN: Yes. Yes, I do see that. Where did I put my hat? And my overcoat, too? Oh, yes, in the hall. Hope I'm not too late. What do you think, Hedda?

HEDDA: Just run, George. Just run.

(BERTHE *comes in from the hall door*.)

BERTHE: Judge Brack's outside, wanting to know if he can come in.

TESMAN: At this time of day? No, no, I can't see him now.

HEDDA: But I can. (*To* BERTHE) Ask the Judge to come in.

(BERTHE *goes out*.)

(*Whispering quickly*) Tesman, the manuscript!

(*She grabs it*.)

TESMAN: Yes, give it to me.

HEDDA: No. I'll take care of it for the meantime.

(*She goes over to the desk and stuffs it in the bookshelf.*
TESMAN *stands, fumbling with his glasses as* BRACK *comes in from the hall*. HEDDA *nods to him*.)

Well, what an early bird we are!

BRACK: Yes, don't you think so? (*To* TESMAN) Are you up and off as well?

TESMAN: Yes. I've got to go over to the aunts. Auntie Rina's dying – well, as good as gone.

BRACK: My dear chap, is she? Then you mustn't let me keep you at such a beastly moment . . .

TESMAN: Yes. I really ought to run. Goodbye, then! Goodbye.

(*He hurries off through the hall door*.)

HEDDA: (*Going closer to* BRACK) You seem to have had quite
a gay time over at your place, Judge . . .

BRACK: Quite a gay time, Madame Hedda. I've not taken my
clothes off yet.

HEDDA: Not you, either?

BRACK: As you can see. But what's Tesman been telling you
about our little evening?

HEDDA: Oh, only something rather dreary about going off
and drinking coffee somewhere or other.

BRACK: Oh, the coffee drinking – I know about that. But
Eilert Lövborg wasn't with them.

HEDDA: No. They dropped him off.

BRACK: With Tesman?

HEDDA: No. A couple of the others.
(BRACK *smiles*.)

BRACK: George Tesman really *is* an innocent, Madame
Hedda.

HEDDA: He's certainly that. Are you getting at something?

BRACK: There is – something.

HEDDA: Well, then. Let's sit down and you can tell me.
(*She sits to the left of the table,* BRACK *on the long side,*
near to her.)
Yes?

BRACK: I had special reasons for keeping tabs on my guests
last night – or some of them, I should say.

HEDDA: Among them – Eilert Lövborg?

BRACK: I must admit – he was.

HEDDA: Now you do interest me.

BRACK: Do you know where he and some of the others spent
the last part of the night, Madame Hedda?

HEDDA: If you think you can tell me.

BRACK: Oh, I think I can tell you. They took part in a
particular live *soirée*.

HEDDA: Of the more sporty sort?

BRACK: Oh, the sportiest.

HEDDA: Do go on.

BRACK: Lövborg had been asked along before. As had the
others. I'd certainly heard about it. But he'd said he

wasn't going at the time. As you know, he's a reformed character.

HEDDA: Living with the Elvsteds, you mean. So he went?

BRACK: Yes, Madame Hedda, the spirit overcame him at my place . . .

HEDDA: Yes. I heard he was overcome.

BRACK: Oh, quite considerably. And, in the process, his attentions rather began to wander altogether. I'm afraid we men don't always stand by the things we say. There it is . . .

HEDDA: But not you, Judge Brack. And Lövborg?

BRACK: Yes, sorry, I'm rambling. The end result was that he ended up in the salon of Miss Diana.

HEDDA: Miss Diana's?

BRACK: Salon. It was she who gave the *soirée*. For a select group of friends and admirers.

HEDDA: Does she have red hair?

BRACK: She does.

HEDDA: A sort of – singer?

BRACK: Oh yes, that, too, among other things. You couldn't help having heard about her. Eilert Lövborg used to be almost inseparable from her. In his old days.

HEDDA: And what happened in the end?

BRACK: Much less agreeable, it seems. From tenderness to outright violence finally.

HEDDA: Against Lövborg?

BRACK: Yes. He accused her – or her friends – of stealing from him. He said his notebook had been taken. That and other things. In short, he stirred up quite a fracas.

HEDDA: And what came of it?

BRACK: It came to – a very ugly brawl indeed with both the men and the women. Fortunately, the police turned up in the end.

HEDDA: The police!

BRACK: Yes. I think it'll be an expensive little carnival for the lashing-out Lövborg.

HEDDA: It will?

BRACK: He put up an almost spectacular fight, if you can call it that. One of the constables got his ear almost crunched in, tunic practically ripped off him and so on. So: it was a case of being marched off to the station.

HEDDA: Who told you all this?

BRACK: The police.

HEDDA: So, that's what happened. So much for wine and roses.

BRACK: Wine and roses, Madame Hedda?

HEDDA: (*Changing tack again*) But tell me, Judge, why do you go nosing around after Eilert Lövborg like this?

BRACK: To begin with, I can't be exactly disinterested if it should come out that the whole incident originated from my house.

HEDDA: Oh, you mean there'll be an investigation?

BRACK: I'm sure. However that may be, I do think that as a family friend, it's my duty to tell you and Tesman about the details of his little night-time escapade.

HEDDA: Oh?

BRACK: It seems pretty clear to me that he intends to use you as a kind of shield.

HEDDA: And how do you arrive at that?

BRACK: We're not blind, Madame Hedda. Just pause a little. Do you think, for instance, that Mrs Elvsted will be going back to her own fireside for a while?

HEDDA: If there was anything going on between those two, there are plenty of other places they could get together.

BRACK: On their own perhaps. Otherwise, every respectable home is going to be closed against Eilert Lövborg – from now on.

HEDDA: You mean, including mine?

BRACK: I can't help saying it would be, well – more than a little painful if this gentleman were to find himself any haven here. If he should try to invade . . .

HEDDA: A triangle?

BRACK: Precisely. It would render me homeless.

(HEDDA *looks at him, smiling.*)

HEDDA: Ah, yes. A roost but no rule.

(BRACK *nods slowly and lowers his voice.*)

BRACK: That is *not* what I've looked for. And I'll see to it that I get what – I have . . .

(HEDDA's *smile disappears.*)

HEDDA: How dangerous you are – when the last bids are made.

BRACK: You think so?

HEDDA: Oh, I've begun to. Now. I'm only thankful you've no hold on me.

BRACK: You're quite right. Just imagine what it could lead to.

HEDDA: Listen to me, Judge Brack. Threatening sounds really don't go with your appearance at all.

(BRACK *gets up.*)

BRACK: How right you are! A triangle is the outcome of natural forces – not compulsion.

HEDDA: Oh, agreed.

BRACK: I think I've managed to say what I meant to. So, until I see you again. Goodbye, Madame Hedda.

(*He goes towards the french windows.* HEDDA *gets up.*)

HEDDA: Are you going through the garden?

BRACK: Yes, it's quicker for me.

HEDDA: As well as the back way?

BRACK: I've nothing against that. It can be almost an attraction.

HEDDA: Even when people are sniping from the inside?

BRACK: (*In the doorway, smiling at her*) Oh, you don't pick off tame little roosters.

(HEDDA *smiles too.*)

HEDDA: Indeed. Not just the one.

(*She sees him off, as they laugh.* HEDDA *stands seriously for a little while, looking out. Then she goes and looks in through the curtains on the back wall. Then moves over to the desk, takes Lövborg's packet out of the shelf and is about to look through the papers.* BERTHE's *voice comes through loudly from the hall.* HEDDA *turns and listens. She hastily locks away the packet in the drawer and places the key on the desk.* EILERT LÖVBORG, *wearing his overcoat and carrying his hat in his hand, bursts through the hall door. He looks somewhat disturbed and excited.*)

LÖVBORG: (*Coming*) I've got to see her, I tell you.

(*He shuts the door, turns, sees* HEDDA, *and regains control almost immediately.*)

You're up!

HEDDA: (*At the desk*) Well, Mr Lövborg. If you've come for Thea, it's a little late.

LÖVBORG: Or for you – a little early. I'm sorry.

HEDDA: How do you know she's still here?

LÖVBORG: The place she's been staying at told me she'd been out all night.

(HEDDA *goes to the table.*)

HEDDA: Did you notice anything when they told you?

LÖVBORG: What, in the way they said it?

HEDDA: As if they were – passing judgement.

LÖVBORG: Ah – judgement! I didn't actually. Tesman not up?

HEDDA: I don't think so.

LÖVBORG: When did he get home?

HEDDA: Very late.

LÖVBORG: Did he tell you anything?

HEDDA: Oh, yes. Apparently you all had quite a giddy time at the judge's.

LÖVBORG: What else?

HEDDA: Else? Oh, nothing – I was so terribly sleepy.

(MRS ELVSTED *comes through the curtains in the rear room.*)

MRS ELVSTED: Oh, Eilert. You're back!

LÖVBORG: Yes – finally. And too late.

MRS ELVSTED: What's too late?

LÖVBORG: Everything . . . I'm finished.

MRS ELVSTED: No, no! Don't say that.

LÖVBORG: You'll say the same when you hear.

MRS ELVSTED: I don't want to hear!

HEDDA: Wouldn't you like to talk to her on your own? I can easily leave.

LÖVBORG: No. I want you here as well.

MRS ELVSTED: I don't want to hear, I say!

LÖVBORG: I'm not talking about the 'evening'.

MRS ELVSTED: What then?

LÖVBORG: Just that; we can't go on seeing each other.

MRS ELVSTED: Not see each other!

HEDDA: I *knew*!

LÖVBORG: I've no more use for you, Thea.

MRS ELVSTED: How can you stand there saying that to me? No more use! Can't I still help you? At least, we must be able to go on working together!

LÖVBORG: I'm not doing any work from now on.

MRS ELVSTED: Then what's left for me?

LÖVBORG: You'll go on living as if you'd never known of me.

MRS ELVSTED: I can't!

LÖVBORG: Try, Thea. Go home.

MRS ELVSTED: (*Digging in*) No. Never! Where *you* are's where I want to be. I'm not letting myself be turned back like this. I want to be here with you – and when the book's out.

HEDDA: (*Softly*) Oh, yes. The book.

(LÖVBORG *looks at her.*)

LÖVBORG: That's right. Our book. Thea's and mine. Because that's what it is.

MRS ELVSTED: It is. You're right. I feel it too. And it's my right – surely, yes? – to be there, at the time . . . I want to be there when you get the respect and honour! And the happiness! The happiness of it, I want to share that with you!

LÖVBORG: Thea – our – book – is not going to see the light of day.

HEDDA: Oh!

MRS ELVSTED: No?

LÖVBORG: It's not possible. It never will be.

MRS ELVSTED: Eilert – what have you done with it?

HEDDA: Yes. *What* have you done?

MRS ELVSTED: Where?

LÖVBORG: Oh, Thea – please – don't ask.

MRS ELVSTED: I must know. I've a right.

LÖVBORG: Very well. I've destroyed it.

MRS ELVSTED: (*Screaming*) Oh no, no . . . !

HEDDA: (*Involuntarily*) But you haven't . . . !

LÖVBORG: (*Looking at her*) Haven't I?

HEDDA: (*Controlling herself*) Well – of course. If you say so. It sounded so unbelievable . . .

LÖVBORG: But – the case.

MRS ELVSTED: Oh, God, God, Hedda – he's destroyed it himself!

LÖVBORG: I've scattered my life. Why not my life's work?

MRS ELVSTED: And this was – the 'evening's' business?

LÖVBORG: I tore it into about a thousand pieces, I'd say. And then I threw them out over the fjord. Right out, into the good, clear, salt water. They can drift. In the current and in the wind. And then they can sink. The same as me, Thea.

MRS ELVSTED: You know, Eilert – with this book – for the rest of my life it will seem as if you'd killed a little child.

LÖVBORG: You're right. It's just like that.

MRS ELVSTED: But how could you? It was mine, too!

HEDDA: (*Barely audible*) Oh, the child!

MRS ELVSTED: (*Breathing heavily*) All gone then . . . Hedda, I'm going now.

HEDDA: You're not leaving together?

MRS ELVSTED: I don't know yet. I don't – see anything much at all.

(*She goes out through the hall door.*)

HEDDA: (*Waits; then*) Aren't you going with her, Mr Lövborg?

LÖVBORG: What – through the streets? And let everyone see her with me?

HEDDA: I'm not quite clear about what actually happened last night. But surely it's not anything that can't be put right?

LÖVBORG: It's not simply last night. It'll go on. And the fact is that I don't want to live that kind of life. Not any more. The – defiance I had, may have had, she's killed off, for me. I can't stop, and turn round, and just say no – to the rest of them. And there it is.

HEDDA: That pretty little ninny's had a whole man in her palm. (*To him*) How can you have so little heart?

LÖVBORG: You can't say that to *me*.

HEDDA: To wade in and lay waste everything you've planted in her life yourself! That's not heartless?

LÖVBORG: You can know the truth of it, Hedda.

HEDDA: The truth?

LÖVBORG: Promise me first – give me your word that Thea will never get to know what I'll tell you.

HEDDA: You have my word.

LÖVBORG: Good. Well then: what I told her was fiction.

HEDDA: About the book.

LÖVBORG: Yes. It's not torn up and it's not thrown into the fjord either.

HEDDA: No? Then where is it?

LÖVBORG: It's destroyed nevertheless. By me, Hedda.

HEDDA: I don't understand you.

LÖVBORG: Thea said it was like killing a child.

HEDDA: Yes – that's what she said.

LÖVBORG: Killing his child isn't the worst thing a father can do to it.

HEDDA: What is worse?

LÖVBORG: Think of a man, Hedda, you know – coming home in the small hours, after an insane, depraved night – coming home to the child's mother and then saying: 'Listen to me for a moment. I've been all over the place tonight, you know the kind of thing. And I had the child with me, our child. So I took him with me and now I've lost him. Lost him – like that . . . Jesus Christ knows where he's got to or who he's with.'

HEDDA: So that's it then? But what you're really talking about, what it is, it's just a book –

LÖVBORG: Just – it was the heart and mind of Thea. Her.

HEDDA: Yes. I see that.

LÖVBORG: So you'll see that she and I cannot go on.

HEDDA: What will you do?

LÖVBORG: Nothing. Just see that's the end of it. Sooner the better.

HEDDA: (*A step nearer*) Eilert Lövborg, listen to me. When you do it – think of perfection.

LÖVBORG: Perfection? (*He smiles.*) All wine and roses as you liked to say . . .

HEDDA: No. That was common of me. I've grown out of
that. But – perfection. Just the one perhaps. Goodbye.
You must go now. And for good.

LÖVBORG: *Au revoir*, Mrs Tesman. Give my love to George.

HEDDA: (*As he goes*) No, wait. You must take a keepsake.
From me. To you.
(*She goes over to the desk, opens the pistol case. She returns
to* LÖVBORG *with one of the pistols.* LÖVBORG *looks at
her.*)

LÖVBORG: That? A keepsake?
(HEDDA *nods slowly.*)

HEDDA: You recognize it? You've been close enough to it
once.

LÖVBORG: That's when you should have used it.

HEDDA: It's yours. *You* use it.
(LÖVBORG *sticks the pistol in his breast pocket.*)

LÖVBORG: Thanks.

HEDDA: Beautifully, Eilert Lövborg. Perfectly. Promise me!

LÖVBORG: Goodbye – Hedda Gabler.
(*He goes out through the hall door.* HEDDA *listens a moment
at the door. Then she goes in to the desk and takes out the
packet with the manuscript, pries into the wrapping, pulls
some of the pages halfway out and looks at them. Then she
goes and sits in the armchair by the stove. She has the packet
in her lap. After a little while she opens both the doors of the
stove and then the packet itself.* HEDDA *throws one of the
bundles in on the fire and whispers to herself.*)

HEDDA: There's where your child is, Thea. With its
beautiful, flowing hair. (*She throws a couple more bundles
into the stove.*) Eilert Lövborg's child. Yours. I'm
burning it. Burning.
(*Curtain.*)

ACT FOUR

The same room at the Tesman house. It is evening. The drawing room is in darkness. The rear room is lit by a lamp suspended from the ceiling over the table. The curtains in front of the french windows are drawn. HEDDA, *dressed in black, paces up and down across the floor in the dark room. Then she enters the rear room and moves over to the left. A few chords are heard from the piano. Then she comes forward again and enters the drawing room.* BERTHE *enters from the right through the rear room, carrying a lighted lamp which she places on the table in front of the corner sofa in the drawing room. Her eyes are red with weeping and she has a black armband on her coat. She goes off quietly and carefully to the right.* HEDDA *goes over to the french windows, pulls the curtain aside a little and looks out into the dark. A little later* JULIANA TESMAN *enters from the hall, dressed in mourning clothes with a hat.* HEDDA *goes to meet her and gives her her hand.*

JULIANA: Well, Hedda, here in such a sad colour. My poor sister has finally given up.

HEDDA: I already knew. Tesman sent a card to me.

JULIANA: He promised me that. But I thought it was up to me to bring you the news myself. In the midst of death, here *you* are –

HEDDA: That was kindly of you.

JULIANA: I'm afraid poor Rina chose a bad time to pass away. When we must all be thinking of the very opposite things.

HEDDA: (*Changing the subject*) Was it – peaceful?

JULIANA: Quite wonderful. Almost a perfect end – if such a thing is possible. And being actually able to *see* George for the last time. Is he not back yet?

HEDDA: No. He said not to expect him straight away. Do sit down, please.

JULIANA: No, Hedda, my dear, thank you. I'd like to, but there's so little time. Things to arrange, the laying out, but I won't tell *you*. But I must see she finishes up properly, as she should.

HEDDA: Is there anything I can do?

JULIANA: You're not to think of it. It's not for Hedda to get caught up with anything like this, certainly not now. Or ever have to think about it, let alone be involved.

HEDDA: That's something one can't always control.

JULIANA: (*Continuing*) There's the world's cycle for you. Sewing of one sort to be done for Rina at my house – and here, soon, quite different sewing altogether. We must thank heaven for *that*.

(TESMAN *comes in from the french windows.*)

HEDDA: I was beginning to wonder when you might come back.

TESMAN: Auntie! You're here with Hedda! Well – now!

JULIANA: I'm on my way. Did you do everything you said you would?

TESMAN: No. I'm afraid I seem to have forgotten half of it. I'll have to go over it with you again tomorrow. My head's so mixed up today. I can't get everything together at all.

JULIANA: Dear Georgie, you mustn't take it like that.

TESMAN: How should I?

JULIANA: You should be glad for the way it has turned out. I am.

TESMAN: Oh yes, yes. You mean about – about Aunt Rina.

HEDDA: You'll be lonely now, Miss Tesman.

JULIANA: Oh, at the beginning I will. But it won't last, at least I hope. Poor little Rina's room won't be empty for long, I know.

TESMAN: Oh? Who are you getting in there? Um?

JULIANA: There's always someone in need – more's the pity.

HEDDA: Could you really bear that kind of cross again?

JULIANA: Cross! God forgive you, child. It's been no cross to me.

HEDDA: But if a stranger should come in now – ?

JULIANA: Oh, you soon make friends with the sick. And I, too, need someone to live for, Hedda. And here, in this house, praise God, there'll soon be something for an old auntie to take care of.

HEDDA: Let's not talk any more.

TESMAN: I say, yes, what a high old time we could have, the three of us, if –

HEDDA: If?

TESMAN: Oh, nothing. It'll all sort itself out. Let's hope so, anyway – um?

JULIANA: Yes, yes. You two must have a lot to think and talk about between you. (*She smiles.*) I expect Hedda has plenty she wants to discuss with you, Georgie. Goodbye now! I must get home to Rina. (*She turns round at the door.*) Good heavens, what a strange thought it is! Now Rina's with me and poor Jochum all at once.

TESMAN: Yes, Auntie, yes, I suppose that's what she is. Um?
(JULIANA *goes out through the hall door.*)

HEDDA: (*Scrutinizing* TESMAN *coldly*) I almost believe this death affects *you* even more than her.

TESMAN: Oh, it isn't only Auntie's dying. I keep thinking about Eilert.

HEDDA: (*Quickly*) Is there anything new?

TESMAN: I wanted to run over to him this afternoon and tell him his manuscript was all right.

HEDDA: So you didn't find him?

TESMAN: No. He wasn't at home. But I met Mrs Elvsted later on. And she told me he'd been here early this morning.

HEDDA: He was. Just after you'd gone.

TESMAN: He's supposed to have said he'd torn the manuscript up altogether. No?

HEDDA: That's what he told me.

TESMAN: He must have been quite demented. And you didn't dare give it him back?

HEDDA: I didn't.

TESMAN: But you told him we'd got it?

HEDDA: No. (*Quickly*) Did you say anything to Mrs Elvsted?

TESMAN: No. I didn't want to. But you should have told *him*. He might do anything in his present state. You'd better let me have the manuscript, Hedda. I'll take it over to him straight away. What have you done with it?

HEDDA: (*Cold and quite still, leaning against the armchair*) I don't have it any more.

TESMAN: Don't have it! What are you talking about!

HEDDA: I burnt it.

(TESMAN *rises, horrified*.)

TESMAN: Burnt! Burnt Eilert's work!

HEDDA: Please don't yell so. The maid will hear you.

TESMAN: Burnt! Good God! No, no, no. It's not possible!

HEDDA: Well, that's how it is.

TESMAN: But do you – have you – any idea what it is you've done! That's no more – less, that's criminal theft! Just think! Just you ask Judge Brack and see what *he'll* tell you!

HEDDA: I think it would be as well not to ask – Judge Brack or indeed, anyone.

TESMAN: But how could you go and do anything so vile! I mean, what was it came over you? Well, tell me! Um?

HEDDA: (*Suppressing an almost imperceptible smile*) I did it for you, George.

TESMAN: For me!

HEDDA: When you came back this morning and told me about his reading it to you –

TESMAN: Yes, well what about it?

HEDDA: When you told me how much you envied what he had done –

TESMAN: But, dear God, that wasn't meant literally.

HEDDA: Perhaps not. But I simply couldn't stand the idea of your being pushed aside.

TESMAN: (*Half doubting, half glad*) Hedda – do you really mean what you are saying? I see that but – but it never occurred to me that you could love me to such an extent! I can't take it in.

HEDDA: Then it's best that you should know now – I *am* going to – (*She breaks off violently*.) No, no – your auntie's the one you should ask. I am quite sure she can tell you.

TESMAN: I think I do know what you are telling me, Hedda! (*She clasps his hands together*.) Is it really true, after all? Um?

HEDDA: I've told you. The maid will hear.

TESMAN: (*Laughing joyfully*) The maid! What a one you are, Hedda! I'm going out and telling her myself.

HEDDA: (*Clenching her hands desperately*) I'm being destroyed!

TESMAN: What is it, Hedda? What are you trying to say? Um?

HEDDA: (*In cold control*) Only that this is all – ludicrous – George.

TESMAN: Ludicrous? That I should be over the moon? Anyway, what does Berthe matter?

HEDDA: Oh, she's very important.

TESMAN: Not for the moment, she isn't. But I think I ought to tell Auntie. I really must! You called me 'George' then. Don't think I didn't notice. Oh, this is going to make old Auntie so happy – it really is!

HEDDA: And do you think she'll also be happy when she hears that I've burnt Eilert Lövborg's manuscript – all for you?

TESMAN: Yes, that's a thought. This manuscript business – I'm afraid we'll have to cover that up a bit, more than a bit. But your doing it for me, Hedda – it would be nice for the old thing to know about that part of it. I shouldn't think it's often that a young wife does something like that all on account of her husband? Um?

HEDDA: Perhaps you should ask old Auntie about that as well?

TESMAN: Well, I certainly shall as soon as I get the chance. (*He looks worried and thoughtful again.*) I can't help still thinking about that manuscript. When you think of it – what a thoroughly frightful thing for poor old Eilert! (MRS ELVSTED, *dressed as she was on her first visit, enters through the hall door. She greets them hurriedly, disturbed.*)

MRS ELVSTED: Oh, my dear Hedda, don't be angry with me for coming.

HEDDA: What has happened?

TESMAN: It isn't anything to do with Eilert Lövborg? Um?

MRS ELVSTED: Yes, it is. I am terribly afraid that there's been an accident. (HEDDA *takes hold of her arm.*)

HEDDA: You think so?

TESMAN: Good heavens, but why is that?

MRS ELVSTED: I heard them talking about him in my lodgings, just as I was coming in. Oh, there are all kinds of unbelievable things being said about him all over the place today.

TESMAN: Yes, I heard a lot of all that. But I can tell you now I saw him go straight home to bed. What about it all!

HEDDA: What was it they said at your lodgings?

MRS ELVSTED: I couldn't find out anything certain. Either they didn't really know, or . . . Anyhow, they just went quiet as soon as they saw me. And I couldn't bring myself to ask them.

TESMAN: We must just hope that you may have got it a little bit wrong, Mrs Elvsted.

MRS ELVSTED: Oh, no, it was him they were talking about. Then I heard something about a hospital –

TESMAN: Hospital!

HEDDA: No, that can't be!

MRS ELVSTED: Oh, I became so afraid for him. So – I – so I went up to his rooms and asked about him there.

HEDDA: Do you think you should have done that, Thea?

MRS ELVSTED: What else was there to do? I couldn't put up with the uncertainty any longer.

TESMAN: But you weren't able to find him either? Um?

MRS ELVSTED: No. And the people there didn't know anything. They said he hadn't been home since yesterday afternoon.

TESMAN: Yesterday! I say!

MRS ELVSTED: I don't see anything else for it. Something awful has happened to him.

TESMAN: Hedda, perhaps I ought to go over and see if I can't find out something?

HEDDA: No, no. You don't want to get mixed up in this.
(JUDGE BRACK, *hat in hand, comes in through the hall door, which* BERTHE *opens and closes after him. He looks grave and greets them without speaking.*)

TESMAN: My dear Judge – it's you!

BRACK: It seemed essential I came to see you.

TESMAN: Auntie's told you the news then?

BRACK: Yes, I did hear that as well.

TESMAN: Pretty frightful, isn't it?

BRACK: My dear Tesman, that depends on how you look at it.

(TESMAN *looks uncertainly at him.*)

TESMAN: Has anything happened then?

BRACK: Yes, something has.

HEDDA: Something – frightful?

BRACK: That also depends on how you look at it, Mrs Tesman.

MRS ELVSTED: Is it to do with Eilert Lövborg?

(BRACK *glances at her.*)

BRACK: What made you think of that? Did you hear something?

MRS ELVSTED: (*Confused*) No, not at all. It's just –

TESMAN: Oh, just tell us what it is that's happened!

BRACK: (*Shrugging*) It seems – Eilert Lövborg has been to hospital. It seems – he's dying.

MRS ELVSTED: Oh God, oh God!

TESMAN: In the hospital! Dying!

HEDDA: (*Involuntarily*) So soon!

MRS ELVSTED: (*In tears*) Oh, Hedda, we left in such bitterness!

HEDDA: (*Whispering*) Thea – there now!

MRS ELVSTED: (*Ignoring her*) I've got to go to him! I must see him alive!

BRACK: There's no point, Mrs Elvsted. No one's allowed in.

MRS ELVSTED: But what happened to him? What was it?

TESMAN: Yes, I mean, he's never tried anything – I mean . . .

HEDDA: Oh, but I'm sure he has.

TESMAN: Hedda, how can you – ?

BRACK: (*Who has been watching her the whole time*) I'm afraid you are the one who has hit on it, Mrs Tesman.

MRS ELVSTED: Oh, no!

TESMAN: (*To himself*) What about that!

HEDDA: Shot himself!

BRACK: Again, Mrs Tesman.

MRS ELVSTED: (*Trying to recover herself*) When was this, Judge Brack?

BRACK: This afternoon. Between three and four.

TESMAN: But I say – *where* did he do it then, um?

BRACK: (*Hesitantly*) Where? Ah, yes, my dear fellow – it must have been in his rooms.

MRS ELVSTED: No, that can't be right. I was there myself just after six.

BRACK: Somewhere else then. I'm not sure for certain. Anyway, I do know that they found him. He had shot himself – through the breast.

MRS ELVSTED: To think of it – ending like that!

HEDDA: (*To* BRACK) You did say – through the breast?

BRACK: I did.

HEDDA: Not the temples?

BRACK: Through the breast, Mrs Tesman.

HEDDA: Yes, yes – the breast. That's good, too.

BRACK: How do you mean, Mrs Tesman?

HEDDA: Nothing.

TESMAN: And you say it's really dangerous then?

BRACK: More than that – mortal. I have no doubt it's already over by now.

MRS ELVSTED: Yes, yes – I can feel it! It's over! All over! Oh, Hedda –

TESMAN: Tell me – how did you find out all this?

BRACK: (*Curtly*) The police.

HEDDA: (*Resoundingly*) At last! Something!

TESMAN: (*Shocked*) Hedda, God help us, what are you saying?

HEDDA: I'm saying – there is beauty in this.

BRACK: Well, Mrs Tesman –

TESMAN: Beauty! What are you saying!

MRS ELVSTED: Hedda, what has beauty got to do with something like this?

HEDDA: Eilert Lövborg has settled up his account. He finally did the thing he should.

MRS ELVSTED: I can't believe a thing like that. What he did was because it was too much for him.

TESMAN: Yes, it was all too much for him.

HEDDA: No, it wasn't. I know it wasn't.

MRS ELVSTED: It was! Of course that was it! Just as when he
tore up the manuscript.

BRACK: (*With a start*) The manuscript? He tore it up?

MRS ELVSTED: Yes. Last night.

TESMAN: (*Whispering*) Oh, Hedda, we shall never see the end
of this.

BRACK: How odd.

TESMAN: (*Wandering about*) Just think of Eilert ending up
like that. And then not to leave behind him the one
thing, the one thing – which would have *continued* . . .

MRS ELVSTED: If only it could be put together somehow.

TESMAN: Just think – if only it could . . . ! One would give
anything.

MRS ELVSTED: Perhaps we can, Mr Tesman.

TESMAN: What do you mean?

MRS ELVSTED: (*Searching in her skirt pocket*) See here. I have
still got the rough notes he dictated to me.
(HEDDA *moves a step nearer.*)

HEDDA: Oh!

TESMAN: So you held on to them! Mrs Elvsted – !

MRS ELVSTED: They're all here. I brought them with me
when I came. They have been in here ever since.

TESMAN: Let me see!
(MRS ELVSTED *hands him a pile of small sheets of paper.*)

MRS ELVSTED: They're in such a terrible muddle. All over
the place.

TESMAN: What about if we could somehow sort them all out!
Perhaps if the two of us could get down to it together –

MRS ELVSTED: Oh, yes! Let's try – at least let's try.

TESMAN: We'll do it. We'll jolly well make sure we do it! I'll
just put everything I've got into it, that's all.

HEDDA: You, George, *everything*!

TESMAN: Well, as far as it is possible to do so. My own work
will have to take a back seat. You do see that, Hedda,
don't you? Um? It's what I owe to Eilert's memory.

HEDDA: I dare say.

TESMAN: So, my dear Mrs Elvsted, you and I must pull
ourselves together. No good, no good brooding over

what's done. We must simply square up and get on with
it.

MRS ELVSTED: Yes, yes, Mr Tesman, I will do everything I
can.

TESMAN: Well, come over here then and we'll make a start
right away. We can really get down to it. What about
here? No, in there, in the back room. You will excuse
us, won't you, Judge? Come along then, Mrs Elvsted!

MRS ELVSTED: Oh, God – if only we can!

(TESMAN *and* MRS ELVSTED *go into the rear room. She
takes her hat and coat off. Both sit down at the table under
the lamp hanging from the ceiling and concentrate eagerly on
the stack of papers.* HEDDA *moves over to the stove and sits
down in the armchair. A moment later* BRACK *goes over to
her.*)

HEDDA: Oh, Judge – what a relief it is: this final business of
Lövborg's!

BRACK: Relief, Madame Hedda? Well, for him it might be –

HEDDA: Not him. For me. To know that someone can
initiate – create – something brave and free that's all
their own. Something perfect, uncompromising.
Beautiful.

BRACK: (*Smiling*) Hm – my dear Madame Hedda –

HEDDA: Oh, I know what you'll say. Underneath it all,
you're a suburban – like, well . .

(BRACK *looks at her steadily.*)

BRACK: Eilert Lövborg's been more to you than you'd admit.
Or am I wrong?

HEDDA: Why should I tell *you*? All I know is that Eilert
Lövborg has had the guts to play the game *his* way. And
he's gone after the biggest stakes of all and he's won a
perfection for himself. Something authentic . . . Beauty.
To do that! And to do it at this stage of it all!

BRACK: I'm sorry, Mrs Tesman, but I've got to wake you out
of that little dream.

HEDDA: Dream?

BRACK: It wouldn't have lasted long, anyway.

HEDDA: Why not?

BRACK: He'd no intention of shooting himself.

HEDDA: No intention?

BRACK: No. The Lövborg business didn't quite turn out the way I told you.

HEDDA: You've held something back? What is it?

BRACK: For Mrs Elvsted's sake – I felt a few white lies were in order.

HEDDA: And they – were?

BRACK: First: he's already dead.

HEDDA: At the hospital?

BRACK: Yes. He never regained consciousness.

HEDDA: What else is there you've not said?

BRACK: What happened didn't take place in his rooms.

HEDDA: That hardly seems very interesting.

BRACK: Not necessarily. Because the fact of it is: that Eilert Lövborg was found shot in Miss Diana's.

(HEDDA *almost jumps up, but sinks back.*)

HEDDA: It's not possible. He couldn't have been there today.

BRACK: He was there this afternoon. He went asking for something he said had been taken away from him. A lot of very strange stuff about a lost child –

HEDDA: Oh! It was . . .

BRACK: At first I thought he might have meant his manuscript. But I hear he destroyed that himself. So maybe he was talking about, what – his wallet?

HEDDA: Probably. So that's where they found him?

BRACK: Yes. There. With the discharged pistol in his breast pocket. The shot had quite – finished him off.

HEDDA: Yes – in the breast.

BRACK: No. It was – lower down than that.

(HEDDA *looks at him in revulsion.*)

HEDDA: That as well! Everything low and absurd and commonplace – why does it cloud over everything I do and touch!

BRACK: That's not all yet, Mrs Hedda. Something also under the heading of 'commonplace', I suppose.

HEDDA: What?

BRACK: The pistol he had on him –

HEDDA: Yes? Well!

BRACK: It must have been stolen.

(HEDDA *jumps up*.)

HEDDA: Stolen! It can't be. He couldn't have!

BRACK: There's no other explanation. He *must* have! Shh!
(TESMAN *and* MRS ELVSTED *have risen from the table in the rear room and come into the drawing room*.)

TESMAN: (*Clutching loads of papers*) Hedda, I can't see a thing under the lamp in there. What about it!

HEDDA: What about it!

TESMAN: Would it be all right if we used your desk for a bit? Um?

HEDDA: Of course it would be all right. (*Suddenly*) No, just a minute. Let me tidy some things first.

TESMAN: Oh, you needn't bother with that, Hedda. There's loads of room.

HEDDA: No, no, it won't take a moment. This can go on the piano just for now. There we are!
(*She has taken something out from under the shelf which was covered with sheets of notepaper. She puts a few more sheets on top and carries the whole pile off to the left into the rear room.* TESMAN *places papers on the desk and moves the lamp from the corner table on to the desk. He and* MRS ELVSTED *sit down and start working again.* HEDDA *returns*.)

HEDDA: (*Behind* MRS ELVSTED'*s chair, ruffling her hair a little*) Well, Thea, my little pretty one. And how is the Eilert Lövborg Memorial coming along?

MRS ELVSTED: (*Looking up at her dispiritedly*) Oh, its going to be such an undertaking – getting any sort of order out of it.

TESMAN: It's got to be possible. It has to be. And putting other people's stuff in order is rather my country, um?
(HEDDA *goes over to the stove and sits down on one of the stools.* BRACK *stands over her, propping himself up against the armchair*.)

HEDDA: (*Whispers*) What was it you said about the pistol?

BRACK: (*Quietly*) That it must have been stolen.

HEDDA: Why do you say that?

BRACK: Because there's no other possible explanation, Mrs Hedda.

HEDDA: You think not?

(BRACK *glances at her.*)

BRACK: Eilert Lövborg was here this morning.

HEDDA: Yes.

BRACK: You were alone with him?

HEDDA: Yes. For a little.

BRACK: You didn't leave the room while he was here?

HEDDA: No.

BRACK: Think again. Weren't you out of the room for even a moment?

HEDDA: Oh – perhaps I was in the hall – only for a few seconds.

BRACK: And where was your pistol case all this time?

HEDDA: I had it in –

BRACK: In what, Mrs Hedda?

HEDDA: In its case – over the desk.

BRACK: Have you had a look to see if both pistols are still there?

HEDDA: No.

BRACK: Well, there's no need to. I saw the pistol Lövborg had on him. I knew it right away from yesterday. And from before.

HEDDA: Do you have it?

BRACK: No. The police have it.

HEDDA: What will the police do with it?

BRACK: Trace the owner – if they can.

HEDDA: Do you think they will?

(BRACK *bends over her and whispers.*)

BRACK: No, Hedda Gabler – not as long as I say nothing.

HEDDA: (*Nervously at him*) And what if you do –

BRACK: (*Shrugging*) You can always say the pistol was stolen from you.

HEDDA: I'd rather die!

(BRACK *smiles.*)

BRACK: That's what people *say*. It's not the same as doing it.

HEDDA: (*Not answering this*) What if the pistol wasn't stolen? What happens then?

BRACK: Oh, scandal, Hedda, I'd say. Wouldn't you?

HEDDA: Scandal!

BRACK: Scandal, that's right. The thing that scares you so much. You'll have to appear in court, of course. You and Miss Diana – the both of you. She'll have to explain how the whole thing happened. Whether it was an accident, whether it was manslaughter, whether it was – homicide. Was he taking the pistol out of his pocket to threaten her? Did the shot go off then? Or was it that she managed to wrench the pistol from off of him, shoot him with it and then put it back in his pocket again? It would be just like her. She's a determined little one, this Diana.

HEDDA: But all this has got nothing to do with me.

BRACK: No. But you'll have one question to answer. Why did you give Eilert Lövborg the pistol? And what will people make of it when it's established you did?

HEDDA: (*Lowering her head*) That's true. I'd not thought of that.

BRACK: Well, fortunately, there isn't any danger as long as I'm quiet.

(HEDDA *looks up at him.*)

HEDDA: You mean you have me in your power, Judge. From now on, you've your own way.

BRACK: (*Whispers softly*) Hedda – dearest Hedda – believe me, I'll not take advantage.

HEDDA: In your gift all the same. In your gift. Unfree! Still unfree! (*She gets up, fiercely.*) No. I *cannot* sustain that. Ever.

BRACK: (*Slightly contemptuously*) Most of us finally get down to the inevitable.

(HEDDA *returns his look.*)

HEDDA: No doubt you do.

(*She goes over to the desk, suppresses an involuntary smile and imitates* TESMAN's *manner.*)

Well then, George? All going well, is it? Um?

TESMAN: Lord only knows. It'll take ages and ages, all this.

HEDDA: (*As before*) I say, what about that? (*She runs her hands lightly through* MRS ELVSTED's *hair.*) Doesn't it seem a bit odd, Thea? Here you are, slogging away with Tesman – just like you did with Eilert Lövborg.

MRS ELVSTED: I only hope I can inspire your husband in the same way.

HEDDA: Oh – it'll happen. In time.

TESMAN: Yes, do you know what, Hedda? I actually do begin to think it's starting to happen a bit like that already. But you go off and chat with the judge.

HEDDA: There's nothing I can do for either of you?

TESMAN: No. Not a thing, thanks. (*He turns his head.*) I think you'll have to see after Hedda from now on, Judge. See she keeps occupied.

BRACK: (*With a glance at* HEDDA) Pleasure.

HEDDA: Thank you. But I'm tired this evening. I'll go and lie down for a little on the sofa.

TESMAN: Yes, my dear. Why don't you? Um?

(HEDDA *goes into the rear room and pulls the curtains after her. Suddenly she's heard playing a frantic dance on the piano.* MRS ELVSTED *gets up from her chair.*)

MRS ELVSTED: Oh, what's that?

(TESMAN *springs to the door.*)

TESMAN: Hedda dear, I say! You're not playing dance music tonight. You've not forgotten Auntie Rina? And there's old Eilert, too!

(HEDDA *sticks her head out between the curtains.*)

HEDDA: *And* Auntie Julie. And the whole lot of them. I'll be quiet from now on.

(*She pulls the curtains to.*)

TESMAN: (*At desk*) She doesn't really like to see us doing this. I know, Mrs Elvsted – why don't you move in with old Auntie! Then I can pop over in the evenings and we can sit and work there. Um?

MRS ELVSTED: Yes. That might be the best thing.

HEDDA: (*From rear room*) I can hear what you're saying, Tesman. But how am I to spend my evenings here?

TESMAN: (*Thumbing through papers*) Oh, Judge Brack'll drop in on you, I'm sure.

BRACK: (*Cheerfully from the armchair*) My pleasure, Mrs Tesman. Every evening. We can be having quite a time, the two of us.

HEDDA: (*Clearly and distinctly*) Yes, you'd like that, wouldn't
you, Judge. Right on top –
(*A shot from the rear room. The three of them start.*)

TESMAN: Oh, she's mucking about with those pistols again.
(*He throws the curtains aside and runs in.* MRS ELVSTED
does the same. HEDDA *is lying lifelessly stretched out on the
sofa. Confusion and cries.* BERTHE *comes in from the right.*)

TESMAN: (*Cries out to* BRACK) She's shot herself! In the
temple! She's shot herself. What about that!

BRACK: (*Half collapsed in the armchair*) God have mercy!
People don't – *do* that kind of thing.
(*Curtain.*)